MEDJUGORJE

and

D1047796

+ MEDITATIONS

+ WITNESSES

+ TEACHINGS

Edited and Published by

THE RIEHLE FOUNDATION
P.O. Box 7
Milford, OHIO 45150

The publisher recognizes and accepts that the final authority regarding the apparitions at Medjugorje rests with the Holy See of Rome, to whose judgment we willingly submit.

—The Publisher

Published by The Riehle Foundation

For additional copies write:

The Riehle Foundation
P.O. Box 7
Milford, Ohio 45150

Copyright©1988 The Riehle Foundation.

Library of Congress Catalog Card No.: 88-062355

ISBN: 0-9618840-5-3

TABLE OF CONTENTS

The concrete cross on top of Mount Krizevac.

DEDICATION

This book is dedicated to Our Lady, our Mother, in thanksgiving for the graces she brings to her children in leading them to her Son, Jesus Christ.

B.R.
The Riehle Foundation

The site of the first apparition on Mount Podbrdo.

PREFACE

The homilies of the Franciscan priests in Medjugorje are becoming a legend in their own time. They speak every day to the thousands who come there. Many different languages are used. Many different nationalities addressed. It's a modern version of the Apostles speaking in "different tongues" to the crowds, following Pentecost.

The homilies are translated, transcribed, and distributed around the world, on tape and in print. They became in great demand through volumes known as the "Gray Book and Blue Book."

This publishing brings you some of the homilies of the priests in Medjugorje during 1987 and 1988. Many of these talks were long, thirty minutes or more. As a result, it was necessary to edit them to conform to the space limitations of print, and to help in the flow and the continuity that is sometimes lost in reducing the spoken word to the printed word.

The publisher takes full responsibility for the transcription and editing. It should also be noted that through translations, some specific words or phrases show slight change.

This book also includes meditations, witnesses and teachings of some American priests, who now add to the growing number of those touched by the Holy Spirit through the "Queen of the Clergy," the "Mother of the Church."

The Riehle Foundation

PART I

Chapter 1

CALL
TO
HOLINESS

Words alone cannot convert the world. If words could have done it, it would have been sanctified long ago. That hasn't happened. So it's our hearts that have to change. St. Paul said, "Preach incessantly." In season and out of season. That means when they like it and when they don't like it. When it's popular and when it's not popular.

So I come to you to try to tell some aspect of Our Lady's messages, knowing that words are not nearly enough. It has to reach our hearts, and that is totally a sovereign act of God. It has nothing to do with cleverness of speech, it is God's touching of our hearts, a call to holiness.

The July 25, 1987 message was Our Lady's Call to Holiness. She said, *I beseech you to take up the way of holiness, beginning today.*

The Gospel reading of today recites the passage of Matthew, Chapter 22. It recalls the great commandment, the flip side of this call to holiness. When they asked Him which is the greatest commandment, Jesus responded, *You shall love the Lord your God, with your whole heart, with your whole soul, and with all your mind.* The second is like it. *You shall love your neighbor as yourself.*

On these two commandments, the whole law is based. God cannot have less than a holy people, because He is all holy.

In the early stages of Israel, God was forming them in what I call a holiness workshop. No nation on earth was able to receive the word of God, because all people on earth were under Satan's power. So God chose Abraham to start a whole new people, whose offspring would be as multiple as the sand on the seashore. It includes you and me. A Redeemer was also promised. Right from Genesis,

> *I will put emnity between you and the woman, between your seed and her seed, and he will crush your head.*

The offspring of the Virgin! God's plan to bring us Jesus Christ, to defeat Satan, to be the teacher of holiness. That makes it truly possible for you and me to be holy. This is very important; that you know that you can be holy. Never accept the opposite lie against this desire for holiness. It is found in Scripture; it is the prototype for holiness.

Our Lady knew it. She knew all of this history. Remember, she is a Jewish Mother. All of her training, all of her spirituality, is not Medjugorje; it is Judaism. Our Lady learned her holiness from a Jewish tradition—the Scriptures. There was no Medjugorje spirituality for her. That is why she asks us to study the Scriptures every day. Everything revealed through Jesus, His Church, the Scriptures, everything He has done for us, we can truly achieve, and thus become "His Holy People."

His whole purpose, throughout the Scriptures was to set up the means to have a holy people.

Medjugorje is private revelation. It will never change or add to the public revelation of the Scriptures. But it is a great stimulus, a great gift of God, that brings us back to Jesus, that brings us back to the Church, back to public revelation. It is an aid to make us that "Holy People."

These gifts of Mary's presence brings such an impulse to holiness that it makes us want to return to Jesus, makes us want to accept His Church, to want to be faithful, to seek holiness. No amount of talking, or sermons, no amount of clever books, could ever accomplish that. No cleverness of human-made wisdom can ever give the desire to be holy. That itself, is a sheer gift and grace from God. That is what is happening here. This beautiful reality that Our Lady knew, this awareness of this call of holiness on her people, through her offspring, Jesus, is realized here.

For I the Lord, am your God, and you shall make and keep yourself holy, because I am holy. (*Lev.* 11:44). God's call to holiness is constantly revealed throughout the messages of the Old Testament, and you can sum up the entire revelation of God's intervention in human history, with one line.

I will be your God, and you will be My people.

It is as if He reveals Himself by stating: I will to be your God, who am a holy God; therefore, I will you to be My people and I can't have anything less than a holy people. It's all part of the Old Testament, a holiness workshop. And from this holiness workshop of the Old Testament, comes the Holy One of Israel, Jesus Christ. And likewise, today, comes Our Lady to reaffirm it all, and you should not forget that Our Lady is a Jewish Mother. She grew up with the Old Testament Scriptures.

She does not come with some novel plan, some new Medjugorje wisdom, some new spirituality. She knows everything of God's Scriptures, from the beginning. She knows God's cosmic plan. She sees it far better than you or I ever could. She's been there. She doesn't have to make references to Scripture, but we do, and we should, so that we can honor the power and impact of what she is saying.

We have lost our roots, our direction. We don't have this sense of a call to holiness in this Jewish tradition, and we need it. So Our Lady comes with a whole series of texts on holiness.

She says, *Without holiness you cannot live.*

She says, *You know I want to guide you on the way of holiness.*

She says, *Live holy lives, live in holiness.*

She says, *Pray daily and change your lives, in order that you may be holy.*

She is totally in harmony with the whole view, the whole plan of God for us to be holy. She says in the message of May 1987,

> *I invite every one of you to start living in God's love. You are ready to commit sin and to put yourselves in the hands of Satan. Decide for God.*

She is the perfect holiness, the Immaculate Conception, and she wants to give to us, God's gift to her—holiness! We cannot be where she is, and with her Son, Jesus, without reaching holiness.

This is an appeal to your hearts. I hope that God can touch your heart with a desire, that you can go out of here saying, "I want to be holy for God. I really want to quit anything in my life that is unworthy of being a servant of God."

Our Lady says she doesn't want Satan to block us on that way, and that we should pray and accept all that God is offering us, on a way that is bitter. Even when there are sorrows, she says. Remember, Our Lady is the Mother of Sorrows. She had terrible sorrows. She knows all about when the way is difficult or bitter. And every one of those sorrows have to be there, because without those sorrows, we cannot really be tested to see if we choose her way to magnify the Lord, to really trust God. And she says,

> *Pray and accept ALL that God is offering you on a way that is sometimes bitter.*

All of her sorrows were tests. It is joys and sorrows together, that lead to glories. The Joyful and the Sorrowful Mysteries lead to the Glorious Mysteries. She says it is God who offers you the sorrows. Don't give Satan credit for the sorrows. Don't give him the credit. We so many times think Satan alone has that credit.

Pray and accept all that God is offering you. God will reveal the sweetness needed, to whomever begins to go on that way of holiness. She knows that.

Whether it's becoming a political refugee who had to flee to Egypt, or searching for Jesus in the temple; whether standing beneath the cross and seeing your Son crucified and mocked, whether it's receiving that precious body that you bore and cuddled, now receiving it broken and bloody and crowned with thorns; contemplating the mystery of all this; she never said it was Satan doing it. She answered all the calls of God. She is totally worthy of the glories she received.

Our Lady tells us this way of holiness means an explicit choice of one master. You can't serve two masters. Heaven is to be longed for; search for it, seek it, seek that Kingdom of God. Your life is short. It will go quickly. Get your values straight. She wants us to see the world from God's viewpoint. Seek it; desire it.

St. Paul states, *It is God who works in us, both the desire, and accomplishment. (Phil.* 2:13).

God gives the desire, and if you truly have desire for holiness, God tends to fulfill it. No mickey-mouse, no play acting, no hypocrisy, no impressing other people. He really wants to make us holy. How the accomplishment part of it will come, that's our act of faith. Our lives are lived between the desire and the accomplishment. God gives the desire, and our life is lived as a pilgrimage, to the accomplishment. And if you aren't sure you have this desire for holiness, then please, brothers and sisters, pray for it. You must desire it. Long for Heaven, don't get stuck on passing shadows.

That road to paradise is not an eight lane freeway. Jesus calls it a narrow path, and few there are that drive that road. That eight lane, that "fool's highway," has a lot of traffic on it. Many there are who drive that road to destruction. We are called to be part of what He calls "the few," who want to drive the way of holiness.

There is an enemy. His name, Our Blessed Mother has never hesitated to use. He exists. She just boldly talks about Satan; whether it pleases people or not, whether it pleases modernists or not, whether it pleases theologians and liberals who think it is some medieval fiction. She says, *I do not want Satan to block you on that way.* She has mentioned his reality many times, as an adversary, an obstructor. Adam's and Eve's record of the fall in Genesis, Chapter 3, is tragically modern, and tragically up to date, always. It is because God made us in His image and likeness, and with it, came a tremendous risk, because He also made us free, free to be subjected to the test. It allows the adversary to do great havoc. It gives him space, so to say.

So our whole way of holiness is a reaching out for God's reality, to reach for that holiness to which He has called us, to let Him work in our life. Our whole pilgrimage of life is summed up in that. Until we see God face to face, we are on a way of holiness to which Our Lady calls us, and to which God, first of all, called His people. Through the intercession of Our Lady, Queen of Peace, may God give us this desire; may He continue to lead us on until we possess Him fully, in His eternal presence, forever.

FR. PHILIP PAVICH, O.F.M.
St. James Church, Medjugorje
Sept. 25, 1987

Chapter 2

SIN
AND
CONVERSION

Words! You know, there have been enough words said and ink spilt to save the whole world, the whole universe, many times over. Words won't save the world, that is not the answer. These messages are not words. We must continually ask that our hearts be touched and opened, so that the word of God, and Our Lady's words, being given to us here, can really affect this change in our hearts.

The primary way for us to spread this message is that we become a message. That my life, my whole behavior, my whole style of living in Jesus, becomes the primary message. The need for all of us is to incarnate this whole reality of conversion and of turning our hearts over to God.

This morning I had occasion to read the first several weekly messages from Our Lady, and I didn't realize that Our Lady had expressed, what she called, "two wishes." In the very first message she said,

> *Dear Children, I have chosen this parish in a special way and I wish to **lead** it.*

Her first wish: I wish to lead it, protect it, and I want everyone to be mine. Then the next week she said,

7

Dear children, in this parish, I want you to start converting...in that way all who come here will be able to convert.

This was the second wish, that people would convert because you have converted. If we could really convert, she says, then other people will be touched or moved through you; instruments of grace.

She also expressed something very touching, that same month, about the sufferings of Jesus. She said that she wanted us to persevere in trials and difficulties, to just think about and ponder how the Almighty, even today, suffers because of our sins. She said the Almighty, her Son, is still suffering, today, now, because of our sins. So when difficulties come, offer them as a sacrifice to God. That's something we have lost today, sacrifice, reparation to the Sacred Heart.

She asked for reparation, satisfaction, for the wounds inflicted upon His heart, and that His heart has been offended by all kinds of sin. Those first weeks of those weekly messages, Our Lady spoke some very profound, elementary truths; her wish that she wanted to lead us, and her second wish that we all convert; and that if we do, then others would actually turn to God because of our conversion.

She also stressed the Heart of Jesus, and how it is inflicted with all kinds of sin. I wish all of you could have the viewpoint of a priest who hears confessions here. You and I are all individuals. I have my own sin history, you have yours. But, for the many hours that I hear confessions here, I can appreciate the variety of Our Lady's expression. *He is offended by all kinds of sins.* All kinds, all types! Thank God you and I are only one. But I think Our Lady has a view none of us can appreciate. She has this view of "all kinds of sins"; that terrible variety of sin that offends the Sacred Heart of Jesus, of her Son.

So she is calling us in a very touching, maternal, compassionate way, to this reality.

Do you believe in sin? Do you?

We always ask: Do you believe in Jesus? Do you believe in God the Father Almighty? Yes! Do you believe in Jesus Christ His only Son Our Lord? Yes! Do you believe in the Holy Spirit? Folks, the belief in Jesus Christ, who became man and died for our sins, is explicit, which brings us to this very question:

Do you still believe in the reality of sin?

This is something we all need to face. Sin is a doctrine of our faith. Sin is an element of the Creed. The existence of sin is a revelation of God. God revealed the quality and existence of sin.

One of my amazements here, as a confessor, is that people are blinded to the reality of sin, and how Our Lady touches them here. They somehow get the grace here, to all of a sudden believe in sin again. There is this great awakening.

I realize this is not a popular subject for preaching, and it is not "in" today. You are not supposed to talk about sin. You know, we all found fault with the Church; "In the old days all they did was talk about sin." But now we have renewal, and we have joy, and we have song, and we have a merciful, compassionate God, and we have certainly taken the focus off of this reality of sin.

Well, here it pops up again. "Do you believe in sin?"

Believing in the reality of sin is essential and correlative to the concept of Jesus, the name of Jesus. When Mary was given the name of Jesus, the Angel said, *Call him Jesus. His name will be Jesus.* In Hebrew, this name meant "God-Saviour," because He will be God saving His people from their SINS. Just think, the moment of the conception of Jesus' reality is linked to the reality of sin and salvation. It doesn't say that He is going to do anything but save His people, "from their sins."

So, if we diminish, if we lose the reality of sin, do you realize you thereby diminish or lose faith in Jesus as a Saviour? Jesus and sin are linked in this particular sense, in that His very function, His very name, His vocational reality, is to save us from sin. Therefore, the Church never allows us to get away from the reality of Jesus, and this linkage and reality of sin.

The very first recorded words of Jesus' ministry, was on the shore of Galilee, where Jesus lived for three years, where He began to announce His theme. It is recorded in Matt. 4:12-17.

Jesus went down to Capernaum, by the sea, to fulfill what had been said through Isaiah the prophet, to heathen Galilee...From that time on Jesus began to proclaim this theme: 'Reform your lives!' The kingdom of heaven is at hand.

He was saying: Convert! Turn back to God! How could Jesus, whose very essence as Saviour is to save His people from their sin, not know His own vocation?

So He expresses in His very first words in public, in His vocational reality, *Reform your lives.* That is, give up sin; I have come to take it away. He was pointed out by John as the one:

Who takes away the sin of the world, the Lamb of God!

John preached repentance and the conversion of sin, a baptism for the remission of sin. John's function as a fore-runner of Jesus, was to Baptize for the repentance of sin; to prepare a people eager to receive, a people who would have clear vision to recognize Jesus when He came. So, when John would say, "Look, there He is! There is the Lamb of God; there is He who takes away the sin of the world; go to Him," they would see Jesus.

There is something happening today, among us, that is very dangerous to the concept of Jesus as a Saviour, and I see this as an evil deception among so many; because we are simply creatures of our day.

Let me put it in a personal context. In the sixties, after Vatican II, I started additional studies at Loyola University in Chicago, in a priest counseling course, a client-centered counseling course. It was the "in thing." From it, I learned that the best thing a priest could do was to have what I call a "go-fer" ministry; a ministry that would mean knowing where to send people, to "go for" help. A supposedly smart priest knew that he couldn't really do anything, but he knew where to go for help. He knew all the resources of the community who could "really" help people. I felt myself getting more and more torn down as a priest.

Part of the emphasis was that in client-centered work, you don't tell people what to do. We were getting the message that "you guys have been deformed in your old theology. You priests have just been dictating, telling people what to do, and you don't have compassion, and you don't understand, etc." The correct concept was that man or woman, left to himself or herself, would always make the right choice; so don't impose your values on people. Folks, I was learning this in the early sixties. That's part of the bad fruit we have inherited in 1987.

This has spread through the whole Church now. Don't impose your values on people. Just leave them alone. Just pick up the feeling, and reflect back to them, and they will make their own correct choice. I remember our professor there had to face his own crisis when one of his clients committed suicide; when the patient didn't make this alleged self-correcting, right choice.

It was implicit in this new doctrine "of the goodness of man," that we have a natural inherent goodness, by which we always choose the correct, the right thing. Gee, my initial Church teaching had always said that man is tilted, because of Original Sin, and that if it is a battle between me and Satan, I'll lose, because he is smarter than I am, he's more clever than I am, and so seductive, that I can't take him on, one-on-one. I'll lose every time. My conscience isn't enough. I need a Saviour, I need someone to team up with, to save me from sin.

So, if you take this new doctrine and run it out to its

consequences, one of the fruits that it bears—that infected convents and priests and infected the entire Church—is that we had all been reduced to "go-fers." And if you didn't have the hyphenated priesthood (if you weren't a priest-dash-psychologist, priest-dash-psychiatrist, priest-dash-social worker, or priest-dash-something) you really didn't have much to offer anybody. Just being a priest of Jesus Christ, and ministering, that really wasn't quite enough. I myself, by 1969, had my own full-fledged vocational crisis, and was ready to sign my name on the dotted line with thousands and thousands of other priests, who were quitting the priesthood.

As I look back, I see now what happened. It is a deformation or bad fruit that has affected us today; a falsehood that you can make up your own mind. No one can tell you what to do. So priests don't even try to form anybody's conscience anymore. That's taboo! Now-a-days, some priests just say that if you really think it is OK for you, if you think birth control, etc., is OK, then it is not a sin for you.

Folks, that is pure poppycock. That is simply not true. No one is entitled to delude themselves in making their own little ivory tower conscience, unaffected by Jesus Christ, and unaffected by His Church and by its teaching authority. If you take that client-centered counseling doctrine, that has infected all levels now, and take it to its logical consequences, then nobody has the right to tell you anything. All they have to do is "be compassionate." If I am compassionate with you, you will make the right choice every time.

Well, then what did we need Jesus for? Why did He even bother to come and save us from sin, if there isn't any?

This blown out of proportion compassion means that just about anything goes today. You can do just about anything, just as long as you have compassion. And compassion then becomes a primary value of lifestyles now. It is in the Church today. Compassion is at the top of the list. It is a high priority value; and because of compassion, you can sleep around, do drugs, get divorced, annulments, homosexuality, go to the

Sacraments, regardless, it's OK, it's between Jesus and you. Follow your conscience. Nobody can interfere with your conscience.

Folks, that is a fabrication, and a destruction of Jesus Christ. That nullifies a Light that came into the world to heathen Galilee. That's like saying leave heathen Galilee alone, just be compassionate, and it will find its own way.

Jesus came to heathen Galilee and started to proclaim this theme: *Reform your lives.* Don't just stick with your own privatised conscience. Reform your lives. He came to tell us what is sin, and what isn't.

There is an objective basis of reality for forming our conscience, and _no_ priest has the right to tell you to do what you want, that it's OK. That kind of high priority value of compassion, can enable anyone to receive the Eucharist, sin or no sin. It says you can't tell people what's wrong in their lives. If that doctrine is true, then how can anybody ever convert? How could Jesus have the nerve to come and say, *Reform your lives?* How dare He come and try to tell me what I should change in my life?

Jesus came to save His people from their sins, and I say, Alleluia! And, I say to you, while you are here in Medjugorje, seek your chance to make a Sacramental Confession. Come with contrite hearts and ask the Lord to show you,

> "Where am I being deluded? What have I been doing in my life that really is not in conformity with the Light of Christ?"

Let Jesus back into the dark spaces of your life. He wants to be the Light, to a Church, a world, a people, that is very much in need of His light. That light will shine in your heart, if we really seek Jesus and His way.

His Mother echoes His words, when she said, *My first wish is to be with you and lead you...you belong to me and my Son.* Her second wish is that you be converted. That is really fundamental doctrine of who Jesus Christ is; and she is His Mother. She _knows_ who He is. She is calling us also to this

Sacramental Confession. It is a big call for some; big changes of lifestyles for some. It is conversion.

I say all this not in any sense of wanting to condemn anybody, for I'm part of the system. It's simply a request to get our act together, examine our consciences against the teaching of Jesus Christ and His Church, not against our own isolated, privatised, conscience. May the Lord come into that, and may He shed His light into whatever in you is heathen Galilee, because He came to be that Light of the world.

FR. PHILIP PAVICH, O.F.M.
St. James Parish, Medjugorje
September, 1987

Chapter 3

THE
FIRST
DAYS

The man who didn't believe in those first days is speaking to you. But now I believe—I very much believe. I would like to tell you why I didn't believe and why I believe now. I would like to invite you and tell you why you should accept this and believe.

Six years, three months and twenty-one days ago Our Lady decided to choose Medjugorje, and to get in touch with the Church. We still haven't recovered from what she did. The children who first saw her were nearly lost when they tried to tell people what they saw. Nobody believed them at first. Later on, however, it was a different picture. To the unfaithful people, Heaven was starting to talk through the apparitions and many miracles. The sun was turning into a shining mass that moved towards the crowds as if it would consume them. People were afraid.

Then the people started listening to the children with their hearts. The children didn't say anything special, except that they saw Our Lady and she blessed them. And she also gave them instructions on a day-to-day basis. That's how the first six days passed.

During that time, various miracles in nature invited people

to come; and many said, "Let's go, let's see the miracles." That kind of curiosity was closing my heart, so I said, "No, that's not Our Lady." But it is interesting that all the school children believed the visionaries. The children were the first to believe. And it is also interesting that nobody was envious of them.

I think back to those days when I didn't believe. At that time I had many reasons for not believing, but now I can sum them up into one: I was too proud.

We cannot come to Medjugorje and say, "I want to pray for grace; I want to show Our Lady that I have my plans to help her, and that they should be approved." Medjugorje is the place where Our Lady invites her children to be obedient, to obey like Jesus.

What does Our Lady want of us? When she came into the Church she said, "Convert." I didn't understand that, even though I thought I did. I thought, like all my parishioners, that Our Lady was finally inviting all who had stopped praying, to start again, that she was inviting drunkards to stop drinking, or those who were destroying family life and Church to stop doing that. The next three evenings I gave three sermons about these things. But nobody converted. Really and truly, nobody. Why? How come that I spoke, and nobody heard?

She came with the message of the meaning of conversion, and she invited us to pray. We prayed for a whole afternoon. Our Lady said that we should pray the rosary every day. The people seemed happy and joyful, and that day they decided not to go home, but to continue in prayer. They all felt that Our Lady was joyful because of our prayer.

That same day, after the Mass and during the prayer, Our Lady appeared in Church. She blessed the gathered people. She was full of joy. Then I said to the gathering, "You who believed were right! Our Lady is really here." The people were glad my faith was awakened. We prayed all night and gave thanks. The people started spreading Our Lady's message to pray, and they intensified prayer in their own homes.

But our prayer wasn't always the prayer of love. Our Lady brought us a message saying, *Don't pray with your lips; when you pray, pray with your heart.* I had trouble understanding that, and Our Lady spoke to me in my heart, and to the visionaries. She said:

> *Today, before prayer, may every one of you forgive your neighbor. Today may everyone find in his heart all of his enemies, and may he show them to the Father with joy. May he pray for them. Let him wish full joy and blessing upon them.*

I thought it was simple.

In the afternoon I told all the people what Our Lady had said, and asked them if they understood me; and all of them said, "Yes." "Can you do that?" I asked. Everyone was silent and it was an uneasy situation, turning into endless desert. I was a little afraid, and I tried to enter that desert with my voice and said, "We will try now to pray for conversion, for the gift of forgiveness."

There was silence for about twenty minutes. It was terribly long. We didn't know where to go.

Then the greatest miracle in Medjugorje that I know of, happened. The church was crowded with people, and one man in the middle of the church shouted with a powerful voice:

"Jesus, I have forgiven!"

And he went on, crying bitterly.

Suddenly, that's what every one of us did. Can you imagine, thousands of people crying, and praying, "Jesus, I have forgiven, forgive me!" Everyone was looking for a hand to squeeze and to say, "Forgive me!" It went on for a long time, and we went on praying rosaries after that. It was an unforgettable prayer.

Our Lady let us experience something that was absolutely new. We felt that a whole new space of prayer was in our hearts. We felt, as if from an immense well, from deep in our hearts, that prayer was pouring out into the world, giving love, joy and happiness. It was the great prayer.

After that, we celebrated the Mass. It was truly a feast of love. We experienced something mystical, something wonderful, as if we were sitting at supper with Jesus. He was present with us on the altar—everybody felt that. The teachings of Medjugorje had begun.

FR. JOZO ZOVKO, O.F.M.
Former Pastor of St. James Church
(from a homily, October 15, 1987)

Crowd gathering for evening Mass.

Chapter 4

THE EXCLUSION FROM THE KINGDOM; THE GOSPEL OF PREPAREDNESS

The Lord is coming in our personal lives and in the world, which we know is a secret known to Him alone. We, you and I, have to be ready. Like the wise virgins in today's Gospel (*Mt.* 25:1-13), we must be ready with oil in our lamps and ready whenever the Lord comes for us. Today's parable has a tragic ending, one of those unpleasant themes in Scripture that tells about those who are excluded from the Kingdom of God.

I was privileged to live in the Holy Land eleven years. I spent two years in the Holy Sepulcher. This old Crusader church, from 1150, has some of those ruins in it and great big Crusader doors. The doors are barred every night at 8:00 in the summer and 7:00 in winter. The eight Franciscans who live inside, and the Greek Orthodox and Coptics and others who live inside this old Crusader basilica, get locked in. Many times, I would go out on some nights when I would go to the prayer meeting at Ecco Homo. I would run back to get in before 8:00 because the doors would be barred. Once they were closed, they were closed. It required opening and closing combinations from both inside and outside to open them.

This Gospel verse has a special meaning to me because I know what it means in the oriental world to bar a door. When you

19

bar a door you literally bar it. They are great big doors and there is no opening them after that. You just don't get in, and there is something terribly final about that. Those are vivid memories for me, running back to get in before the door closed.

Jesus is called, in the Book of Revelation, *the one who opens and no man shuts; the one who shuts and no man opens.* There is a terrible finality about that verse in the Gospel.

The theme of five foolish virgins and the five wise virgins symbolizes the Christian community as a whole. It really has an aspect for us to take seriously. In the Christian community there are foolish and wise people. There are those who will be ready and there will be those who will not be ready. That is already a bit of a sobering message. It is not pagans that are the five foolish ones, nor those who do not believe in Jesus. Notice, they cry "Lord!" They know the Lord. They are people who know Him already, people who know Him and are familiar with Him. These are people who are in the Christian community who hear that horrible message, *I do not know you.* You are locked out. It is a combination theme of preparedness. It is living in union with the Lord and having the oil of Sanctifying Grace (the Holy Spirit), combined with the terrible theme of the Gospel—exclusion from the Kingdom.

Let this be a day of our hearing Our Lady's message, the Queen of Wisdom. She is not teaching us to look for signs. She is not teaching us to scan the skies to see when Jesus will come so that we will be ready. Notice in the parable, all ten virgins fall asleep. It is not like five are awake and five fall asleep. It is not like five are ready and five are not—five have the oil of the Holy Spirit and five of them do not. Again, it is not meant to say half will be saved and half will be lost. Jesus also has some difficult passages about the narrow path and the wide path and the many who walk it to destruction, and those few who seem to find the narrow path. We are caught in a time of having to be prepared and to just go on living our lives.

Pope John XXIII had a beautiful verse that I always liked: "Any day is a good day to be born, and any day is a good day to die." Falling asleep means you go on living your life—

any day is a good day to die. Some of the saints have been asked what is a good way to prepare for death? Just do what you are supposed to be doing, but be ready. You will have the grace, you will be able to light your torch and enter immediately when the bridegroom comes.

But at the last minute, those without oil in their lamp, those who are not ready, those who do not have this grace, this favor, and have neglected it, may be caught short. It is an awful thought, but these are Jesus' words, not mine.

We must go on living our lives being ready. Our Lady is trying to teach us that. So many people only look for signs and wonders. How do we know when He is coming? There is a whole element of the Christian body so concerned about the Second Coming, reading signs, political moves. How soon will the Lord come? We are taught to be ready and Our Lady has asked us to decide for God, to decide for Paradise. *Dear children, start living in God's love.* Get that oil in your lamp and be ready.

You can go on living your lives. You do not have to worry. For 150 weeks Our Lady gave Thursday messages, enlarging those five key words. But of those 150 Thursday messages, none of them had alarm in it. None were scary, eschatological kinds of things. They were all on faith and conversion; they were all about getting oil in your lamps, staying in grace and living for God. You do not have to worry; you do not have to be afraid. She started us in this school of holiness, of preparedness.

My dear people, brothers and sisters in Christ, let us ask for this grace to take the Lord seriously, not to waste our time, but to buy the time, as St. Paul says, to be ready and to live our lives in calm and peace and in possession of ourselves, because we are living in the peace that is the reality of the Spirit's presence in us.

We do not have to hurry and scurry around today worrying about signs and when He is coming. Just be ready. Go on with your life, be at calm and be ready, though, when He comes. When the cry goes out, our love will indeed be illumined with the light of the Spirit that is there. We've got the pilot light inside, and it will turn on full of light and go with the Lord.

Let us beware of false compassion, false compassion which allows people to live in sin, because we've got a big merciful God. I have heard that so many times. Hearing confessions here for months has been a real revelation as to what is going on in the Church. These are people in the Church, not pagans; these are people in the Church who will try to get in and say, "Well, we were Catholics. Our priest told us we could do this." These are people in the Church. This is the scary part of it. They will try to get in on the fact that, "I am Catholic. I ate and drank with you." Do you know how many people are drinking foul and false communions—receiving Communion unworthily—and have been doing it for years, in bold and stark sin? They continue coming to eat and drink with Him and He is going to say, *I do not know you.* "I was not in union with you." That is a scary reality.

I invite all of you today to watch out for false compassion. It is a sickness in the Church today. It is a sickness in the priesthood, and it is a sickness in our people. It is a compassion that allows people to live in sin, and nobody is telling them the truth.

May we all hear the truth from our priests and may we all want to live the truth. May we all want to be faithful, not kidding ourselves, not changing the names of sin for lifestyles and optional versions of living, and for all that hides the fact of that horrible reality. May the Lord have mercy on us, and may we really hear the words of this Queen of Wisdom, who is calling us to convert, to repent.

Keep that oil in your lamp, so that you will never hear those horrible words, so that you will be ready to go in with Him and rejoice forever as that risen, redeemed, forgiven people. The Lord loves sinners and He has compassion and mercy, but it is for *repentant* sinners, not for sinners who deny that they have sin.

FR. PHILIP PAVICH, O.F.M.
St. James Church, Medjugorje
(homily at the English Mass, Nov. 8, 1987)

Chapter 5

CHOOSE YOUR KING

My dear brothers and sisters, I was asking myself this morning, going from the church to the rectory, and the rectory to the church, if there is a proper word to be said here and now, about all the sacrifices which you have to endure today and in these times. And there is no such word to be said which would relate in a proper way. These words, which will be said here, let them somehow be a possible reflection of these times, but first of all let God speak, and I pray and ask for the guidance of the Holy Spirit that my words, and your words, never stand between us and God. Let them be a help for God's communication to us and let this pilgrimage be a help, that God might speak to all of us.

A few days ago, we were celebrating a great day of our faith, "Christ The King" and I think it is the proper moment to reflect upon this. What does that mean in our faith, to have Christ as our King?

If you go back in the Old Testament, you will see something special in the way God chooses the leaders for His people. There were eight children, and surprisingly, the youngest was chosen to be king of Israel, of the chosen people. It was David, the youngest, who you would never guess to be the

23

choice. This relates to our own attitudes and feelings in a very special way. You see, we think other people would be chosen, to be special, to be sent, to be kings, anointed, blessed, gifted. We think this about others, not so much about ourselves.

Christ the King is telling each and every one of us today, that we are all chosen, and that you are chosen, in a most special way. You are called by name. You are that special person. Christ the King relates to you, and He chooses you, even if you feel the youngest, or the least important, nothing special. Have respect for yourself. Don't bring yourself to just anywhere, where any kind of sin could put you down; don't put yourself in a sinful situation, in a degrading situation—because you are chosen, precious. Respect what you are. Continually, here in Medjugorje, we experience that the visionaries are not the only ones chosen. The pilgrims, the priests, the parishioners, everyone is chosen.

If you read the Gospels, you will see that when the king was to depart, he left his property in the hands of some other people, and when the time came for him to take it back, he sent his servants to take what belonged to him. But, the servants were killed. Finally he sent his only son to take back what belonged to the king, to the father. They also killed the son. In the Old Testament, we have the prophets being killed, and at the end—Jesus being killed.

You see, we have a problem; we can't stand on our own. God has to come and take us for Himself. We belong to Him by our nature, we are His property. So God continually sends His prophets, His people, His messengers. At the end, He sends His Son, who also was killed—crucified. And this is your and my own story. God is always sending His messengers because He would like to bring us home. We belong to that home. But we continually choose to kill; in different ways, in different times. In our times, that crucifixion is being traumatized in a most dramatic way—abortion.

His crucifixion is a kind of reception. God wants to find love in our hearts, in our lives. This is the kind of relationship God wants to develop with us, but He continually receives this wrong kind of reception in our lives. The King continually asks to come, but He continually receives this same kind of reception. Still, the King, continually loves us. Even though He receives this kind of reception, rejection, He still continues loving. The Father continued sending His prophets and in the end His Son. And His Son showed His love—on the cross.

So now, it is a choice you and I have to make. Who do you take as your own king, your leader? Someone about whose love you are not sure? That might be a person, a possession, material wealth, anything of the world. But one way or the other, we do choose our king. What will be the way of our thinking? And when we choose one, we reject the other; but, we have to make our choice. And, we continually choose our king, every day.

You don't have a choice about choosing or not choosing your king. You must choose.

We celebrate this great feast day of Christ the King at the end of the liturgical year, where the King was born first, grew, where He spent those years with His disciples, with us; where He gave us the teachings, and then He was crucified, all this to show this profound love. Then He rose from the dead, and only then was He able to take His throne, to take His position of leadership. By His deeds and words, He thus deserves this place, this kingship.

Choose the king about whose love you are sure; about whose love you can't make a mistake. And, this pilgrimage, every step of it, every experience, every sacrifice, is meant to help you choose your king. Actually, the sacrifices you have to endure on this pilgrimage helps you to leave everything else aside, especially the false king that doesn't mean well, that leads you nowhere, that brings you trouble.

On this pilgrimage you are climbing the hill of the cross with the real King, entering the Holy Family of Bethlehem, symbolized by the hill of the first apparitions. You enter, stay and live with that family, here, in the church. With that King you climb the hill of the cross. The term "Mystical Medjugorje" means the very geography of this place. It speaks to you about the reality of our faith, our life. It shows us the map of life, the way. But first of all it shows us how to choose our king, our leader, how to find the real priority in our lives.

So, this pilgrimage is not so much a time to search for a particular place, or person; or see something of a physical nature, or hear certain words. This time is especially for you to search for that king of yours; to search for that leader of your life; to literally search for your own self, for your values, your own purpose. This is what Medjugorje is.

Here, we come to that most important message of Medjugorje—''Conversion.'' It is not an event of a single day, a one time thing. Medjugorje is a place of direction, the way to go, the road map. It is not a time or place at which to stay, but just a place along the way. Conversion is every time you forgive, when you reconcile. Conversion is trying to see in your brothers and sisters what God Himself sees. Conversion is to become like God in attaching His attitude of thinking and behaving.

One of my experiences here, was to see that some of the people who became the most active in spreading the message of God and the Gospel, are the kind of people I would never, never choose to do that. Because, I would never recognize the beauty that was in them, the power, the strength.

But God was able to see that beauty in them, because God knows what is in you. So if you are willing to cooperate with God, He will get the best out of you.

You and I are like the ground, the earth. When it's too cold, frozen, it can grow nothing. It is a dead ground. When there is no water, only heat—sin—it can grow nothing. When a little sunshine comes, a little rain—growth. It becomes beautiful. Allow God to bring His sunshine and water into your heart so that you are able to grow the most beautiful flowers, whose seeds are there, with you—I assure you.

That is the experience of Medjugorje. God is willing to accomplish miracles through you, only if you allow Him, if you allow Him to become your King, and your Leader.

Medjugorje is facing the reality of life, and that is conversion, every day.

Thus we have to choose; to forgive when we feel there is no sense of forgiving; we have to fast when it's too difficult; we have to pray when we feel it just isn't a time to pray. When you participate in Mass in your parish, with a pastor or fellow parishioner you don't like, then it is the time of conversion. It is the time to choose God as your King. It is the time to choose to climb the hill together with Him, to enter that family.

So here at this place, this place is asking for nothing, has no demands, no expectation, puts no pressure on you. It just gives you the opportunity to find the priority in your life; gives you the choice to choose your king.

Our Lady is simply asking all of us, "Go home and do whatever He tells you, wherever, and however, He tells you." Choose your King.

FR. SVETOZAR KRALJIEVIC, O.F.M.
A message to pilgrims
Nov. 24, 1987
St. James Church, Medjugorje

Chapter 6

YOU MUST CHOOSE.
DECIDE FOR
PARADISE

We believe these messages are from Our Lady. Sorry to say, there are some, and even our local Bishop, for whom we ask you to pray, and to pray with us for these apparitions to be approved. We must come with a true, obedient, attitude toward the Church; that the final decision of the Church authorities will pass judgment on the authenticity of the apparitions. We appreciate the fact that you are here; and are willing to seek, willing to hear, willing to try to open your hearts to Our Lady's messages.

That's a gift. It is a gift to me personally; it's a gift to the people sitting next to you, and all of us in this Church. We are God's people and the more we yield ourselves to God's purposes, the more we actually benefit one another, the total Body of Christ, and all mankind. We are indeed meant to be the light of the world and the salt of the earth, as Jesus told us.

So, your wanting to enter in, is a true gift to the Church, and it is for that reason that Our Lady always thanks us. It is a decision that's involved, even as she said in this message. The Lord seeks us to really decide for His Kingdom and for Himself. The third level of the messages is very important, and that is the very presence of Our Lady herself. So many times people have asked me if there was an apparition last night, and what did she say? Like they were looking for a daily message of some kind.

She came last night. That is the message. The message is her presence with us. The message is that she continues to be with us. She is a mother who is with us, as Jesus is with us. The text of Is. 7:14: *Behold the virgin shall conceive and bear a Son and His name shall be called Emmanuel,* which means God with us. Jesus is the offspring of that Virgin, God with us! And His mother, is the mother who is with us.

If you see Mary and Jesus in the light of St. Paul's reading last Sunday, as the "New Adam," you see that old Adam, so to say, failed us. The New Adam was totally faithful and brings us to life as new creatures in himself. The old Eve can be pictured with the serpent wound around her neck, as it were; the New Eve has the serpent under her feet. She never came under his power. That is why she is Immaculate. She is that woman without sin, and she is the Mother of all the living. As the New Eve, the Mother of all the living could do nothing less than be with us always; bringing us alive in Christ her Son, Who is the very Emmanuel—God with us.

That is a wonderful theme all by itself. Jesus and Mary as the New Adam and the New Eve, and we as the blessed offspring that are brought to life. Mary is the Mother who is with us. It is a great gift, and she sees that. She has thanked the Lord in several messages and alluded to what a joy it is for her to be allowed to be with us in this special, prolonged, continuing presence. So there is a very special aspect to her presence. In fact, that part of the messages—her daily presence, her being with us—is the only new thing at Medjugorje. Everything is well-known and well-heard. Faith, peace, conversion, prayer and fasting. That is Gospel. These are the words of Our Lord, Jesus, her Son.

So the fact that she should repeat these most fundamental Christian truths is not surprising. The unique and novel element is that people, like yourselves and literally millions of others, have come and want to embrace these very household words of Sacred Scripture. Her presence and her holiness is making them a power. Her presence makes the difference, so that people really do want to pray, have a desire to pray, have a desire to fast, a new power to convert and turn to the Lord Jesus, the Blessed Fruit of her womb; and come alive in this Mother of all the living, come alive in her Son. So we rejoice in Our Lady being with us; that she has been able to stay with us this long.

So the extension of these basic fundamental message words is the extension and refinement, and filling-in, of the base message through these weekly, and now monthly messages. But above all, accept Mary, herself; accept her person as the most basic message. She really is, herself, the message.

This was last month's message, of October 25, 1987:

> *My dear children, today I wish to invite all of you to decide for paradise. The way is difficult for those who have not decided for God. Dear children, decide and believe that God is offering Himself to you in His fullness. You are invited and you need to answer the call of the Father who is calling you through me. Pray, because in prayer each one of you will be able to achieve complete love. I am blessing you and I desire to help you so each one of you might be under my motherly mantle. Thank you for your response to my call.*

Having received some 150 Thursday messages, and before this one, nine monthly messages, I was personally struck by Our Lady's salutation, "MY Dear Children." Every other message said, "Dear Children." I looked back through all the messages and found that this is the first time she used, "My Dear Children."

Now that's not to be made a big deal of, but I found it very touching. It has a warmth about it that is connected especially with the word about the mantle. There is a tie-in of Our Lady's care and concern for us, in a very special way in this message. Maybe that is why that word "My" occurs, for what I believe, is the first time in over 150 messages. And if you think of the line in the message:

> *I am blessing you and I desire to help you so that each one of you might be under my motherly mantle.*

You see, it is "MY Dear Children," I want you "...under my motherly mantle."

In Jerusalem, there is the beautiful Church of the Visitation. On the wall are great big paneled paintings, and one of the paintings is titled, "Refuge of Christians." It shows Our Lady with this great big mantle, and all kinds of nice black people, white people, yellow people, all kinds of representatives of the human race under this huge protective mantle. The "Refuge of Christians," the New Eve who wants to bring us all alive in her Son, Jesus Christ, the New Adam. Just think, Our Lord Jesus Himself used this very loving feminine image, His Mother.

There, also, at the Mount of Olives, is a little tear-drop church overlooking Jerusalem, and recalls the text of Jesus' Palm Sunday entry into Jerusalem (*Lk.* 19:41) *As he saw the city, he wept over it saying, If you only knew the path to peace,* which of course, is Jesus Himself. Like, if only you knew Me. I am the way. I am the life, the truth, I am the path to peace.

But now it is hidden from your eyes and your enemies will hem you in, cast you down and not leave a stone upon a stone within you, because you did not know the time of grace. The visitation of grace, the time of the visit; they did not recognize Jesus.

Go back to the beginning of the message. She says,

> *Today I wish to invite each one of you to decide for paradise.*

She wants us to *decide* for Paradise. We accept the fact that we are in exile, and you must really accept that fact; it is part of our revealed faith. You are not in Paradise, no matter how good you think you have it. We are in exile. What you call home and what you think is comfortable, just happens to be the place on this mother-earth-surface where you are spending your personal exile. Home is Paradise! What God created us for, to be in His image, to be free from sin and death (which we lost), that is what we're deciding for. Our Lady, as the New Eve, knows all about the old Paradise, for as soon as Adam and Eve lost Paradise, she came on the scene.

I will put enmity between you and the woman. She is that woman! She is to open up Paradise for us by bearing the one who will crush Satan's power. She knows very well that you are not there yet. We must never forget this, no matter how good we've got it. We're not there yet, and it really takes a decision. *Deciding* for Paradise also means we are *deciding* to live for the Kingdom of God. Wherever Paradise is, there is God's presence. Seek first the Kingdom of God.

She says, *The way is difficult for those who have not decided for God,* for the Kingdom, for Paradise.

Those who have not decided, that's a heavy burden; the dissension, depression, problems, violence, all kinds of trouble, the lack of true peace. That is the true lament of Jesus over Jerusalem. They didn't know Him; didn't decide for Him. She uses the word "deciding" three times here.

Decide and Believe. Decide for God AND believe it. This really requires a faith decision. God so loved the world that He gave us His only Son. He couldn't give us more than that. Our Lady says that, *You are invited.* Those words ring a whole bunch of Gospel bells. The parables of invitations; to the wedding banquet, to the different feasts in Jesus' parables.

You are invited. And you need to answer the call of the Father, who is calling you through me, she implies. She is saying very clearly; God is sending me, and you need to respond to me, because as you respond to me, you respond to the One Who sent me. Jesus, Himself, says those same words more than once in the Gospels.

It's like this exile image. People seem very concerned with making it big in exile. Have bigger homes, bigger cars, bigger city, bigger salaries, millionaires. They are making it big in exile. Is that your goal? You will have to decide.

Fool, your soul will be required of you this very evening, the Gospel passage says. Jesus' words echo back. Oh, we need to enter all right. We need to enter, to respond, to decide. All of our needs today, the world's needs, those are all psychological crutches, the need to be somebody. They don't tell us about "Our God Needs," our need to save our soul. What can you give in substitution for your soul? Dear children, you need to answer all right, because your whole purpose of existence depends on your answer. It depends on these kinds of decisions, deciding for God, deciding for Paradise; because the way is difficult for those who do not.

Jesus Christ, the Son of God, wept tears over those who did not know the time of the visitation. It is a mother's love and a Saviour's love that wants to tell us the truth. No mollycoddling, soft, watering down, but the tough, true, caring love, that is truly for our benefit.

Then she says, *Pray, because in prayer each one of you will be able to achieve complete love.*

Prayer, again, is our chief responsibility. It is the flip side of loving God with our whole heart, soul, mind and strength. Recall that first of the great commandments. It is not; if you like to do it, or feel like doing it; it is a command of God, to love Me as your God. It is relating to Him, or praying to God with your whole heart, mind, soul and strength.

He who loves me keeps my commandments, Jesus said. Notice that love is contingent to obedience, to deciding. Therefore, Our Lady addresses this word, "decision." Never once did she talk about feelings, emotions, enthusiasm. God didn't ask you to have any emotions about loving Him, He just said, DO IT!

Today, if we don't answer to our feelings, we're not authentic, mature. They tell you, if you don't feel like praying or going to Mass then don't go. If you're not honest with yourself, you're not an authentic person. Praying with the heart means deciding to do it, to commit to it. Let the Lord take care of your feelings. *You shall love your God with your whole heart.* It is the same expression. Our Lady is very Biblical.

So it is in prayer then, in this deciding, that we can truly exercise love, and achieve a dimension of God's love in our lives that she calls "complete." We can enter into this complete love by obeying the Lord. Try to see these messages in Biblical terms. It is my impression that almost all of these messages have to be understood in light of Sacred Scripture. We need to interpret them in this fashion, to see the richness of these messages.

The Seat of Wisdom, I believe, is speaking to us. I believe she is sent by the Father to speak to us, and this is another one of her heart messages. The mother who loves, is with us, speaking fundamental, wonderful, Biblical truths.

FR. PHILIP PAVICH, O.F.M.
St. James Parish, Medjugorje
November 25, 1987
(speaking on the October 25, 1987 message.)

Chapter 7

I LOVE YOU IMMEASURABLY

Very often I speak about three levels of the messages of Medjugorje. You have the main message, and these are prayer, conversion, peace, fasting, penance, faith; and they are like guidelines in all the happenings here at Medjugorje. So if somebody asks *why* the apparitions at Medjugorje, you can tell them Our Lady is inviting us to peace. And if people ask you how do you get to that peace, then the answer is, through conversion. And if they ask you, what must we do then, you have the three other answers—pray, fast and have faith. So this is the main structure of all the happenings here.

And then we have other messages, the so-called Thursday messages, and those given on every 25th of the month. And in these messages Mary indicates to us what it means to have peace, what it means to convert, what it means to pray, etc. Because of those Thursday messages and those given on the 25th, we can speak about the "school of prayer" that Mary has opened here; because in the messages she keeps giving us new indications, and new impulses. If you read all these messages, you would say there is nothing new, and that is true. There is nothing new.

But there is only one message of Medjugorje, and this is

35

a very new one; and that is Mary's daily presence. This is a message that does make everything new and different, her presence here; because this certainly isn't the first time you've heard the words peace, convert, etc.

But now many people accept these things in a new way. And this you can only explain because Mary is really present here—in a very special way, a daily way. Through her presence, she has created this new atmosphere in which people can accept all the things now, in a new light.

So you have the answer to "why apparitions?" She's not here to bring us something new, but to teach us to do what we already know, in a new way, in step by step direction.

I believe many people have difficulty in accepting apparitions in general, because they don't know why God is giving us this. And if somebody tells me, "I don't accept Medjugorje," then I ask what is it that you don't accept. If you accept peace and prayer, conversion, fasting, faith, then you have accepted everything.

This is what Mary really wants—and I believe many people have made a mistake in their methods. They said, "We're going to wait until the Church has approved." What is it that the Church must approve here? Peace? Conversion? Prayer? Faith? All this has been approved of already. But we have forgotten much, and God, through Mary, wants to give us this input. If someone says, "I don't accept this input because I live all this already," then he's completely right. The main thing is that we really begin to do what we already believe.

The only thing that can be said for certain is that after the visionaries told us they were seeing Our Lady, then a renewal began to happen. And the renewal is the last reason, or criterion, to accept anything like this in the Church. So what you are going to hear in this last message is that she comes to give us input for those main messages, as we said before. It is a new instruction in this school that Mary has been guiding for seven years.

First of all, we have the words *My dear children*. I believe that through these words, she wants to repeat that she is a mother. And this is a confirmation of the teaching of the 2nd Vatican Council. She was declared Mother of the Church, Mother of all of us.

Vicka, in answering a question of how she would prefer to address Mary, said, "Mother—because when you look at her, you have the impression she wants to embrace the whole world and save everybody."

She invites us again to surrender everything completely to her. I say very often we have become specialists in burdening ourselves. Many worries of tomorrow, we carry them today; and very often we become incapable of facing today, because we are tired of yesterday and afraid of tomorrow.

If we look at Medjugorje from this point, then we can say that Mary really wants us to live for today. She wants us to free ourselves every evening from all the burdens of the day. She wants us to have the strength to live today.

This is really the reason she told the parish to meditate on the passage of the Gospel of Matthew 6:24-34. In it you have three important points.

1) Jesus says you cannot serve two masters.
2) Why have fearful worries.
3) And with your worries, you cannot make your life better or longer, but search first for the Kingdom of God, and all the rest will be given to you.

I believe we can do this every day. This is the sense, and the reason, why we pray in the evening. The prayer of the evening is always a prayer of liberation. This is the moment when we give all the good things and the bad things to God.

When we look at everything we consume, like television or the news we receive during the day, the conflicts we go through, etc., all of this goes right into our soul; and it's a burden, it's heavy. Our psychological level is overburdened by so many things. Mary invites us to surrender everything to God, through her. Mary wants us to do this every day. Of course it is not easy, but if we practice it every day, we will succeed in doing it. Then we will understand what the meaning of peace really is, and we can do much for that peace.

When she says, "start," we are not being asked to carry the wars taking place in the world, because we can easily say I can do nothing about it. But we can do so much where we are, in surrendering the weights and burdens we carry around, and the encounters we have with others.

Then she said, *This is the only way I can present every one of you to God.*

That means, if we are prepared to surrender everything to her, then she can present us to Him; she is a mother who is offering. She presented her Son Jesus in the temple, a helpless child, and He allowed her to offer Him. The second time she offered Jesus to the Father was on Mt. Calvary. It was the same Mother. She did not go up to Calvary to watch who was doing evil things to Jesus. She went with Him to offer Him up again, and for us. It is important to know this, because Mary is prepared to be always with us, and offer us, as well.

Then she said, *I love you immeasurably.* This is something she has repeated more than once. She is a loving mother. On the paper, the written message is just a word, but the more we fast and pray, I believe this word can become our life.

She talks about our freedom, twice; and she explains her attitude toward our freedom. She respects it, with love, and in her humility, she submits to it. We could speak a lot about our freedom. For me, personally, it was always one of the biggest problems I found here, in the happenings, and I am thinking of the visionaries. Perhaps many of you thought like I used to think: If somebody sees our Lady, they must become holy immediately. I really had to learn that this was not the case. They did not have to continue. I did not understand their freedom to choose, but they are really free. And they are not that happy about it either. Maria told me just after she wrote down the message, "I am not so happy that I am so completely free. But it's really true."

God respects this freedom with love. It is a very big gift for us, and of course, our freedom does not exclude our responsibilities. This is certainly a big problem with many people today. Many think we are free so we can do everything we want. This is why we have so many problems. But Mary says it once again in these messages, "It is your free decision." She does not want to force us in any way. I believe this is what can save the visionaries, though I understood it very slowly. For if they had been under pressure to do what they are doing, then after six years we would have fanatic people by now; or spiritually very sick people. This is why Mary respects our freedom with so much love.

Still she does everything she can to move us positively in our freedom. It is quite clear she is the humble servant of God, here also. She said through Jelena, more than once, *I knock at many hearts, and many hearts do not open. Pray so that they can all open.* So you see, she is not happy if through our freedom, we destroy ourselves. But all she can do is knock at the door of our hearts.

She also speaks about her plans for us and the parish, and our need to pray, to pray a lot for recognition of these plans. She says that, *Satan is here also, and he tries to do many things.* She speaks of his deceptive strength, and that should be underlined. This is part of the education Mary is giving to us. Do not let this *deceptive strength* of the devil lead you into a mistrust of God, or yourself.

There are many positive things in every single one of us. If we really become aware of them then we have begun to go on Mary's way.

Mary loves us just the way we are, here at Medjugorje, or wherever we are. She says, "immeasurably so."

FR. SLAVKO BARBARIC, O.F.M.
St. James Parish, Medjugorje
November 27, 1987
(homily given on the meaning of the message of Nov. 25, 1987)

Chapter 8

THINK ABOUT IT

We have to ask ourselves why apparitions? And we have to try to find the answer for us personally. On the third day of the apparitions, Our Lady came and said, *Peace, be reconciled, Peace!* Think about it.

This is Our Lady's intentions throughout all the years. She wants to help us to find peace. I believe through the key word, "peace," we can understand and hear many things. But you must understand peace in a biblical sense. Peace means peace with God, reconciliation with God. After we have that peace with God, then we can begin to have that peace with others. So the alternative to that peace is *not* a war; the alternative distraction is sin. For that reason we are invited to conversion.

The second main message of Our Lady here is conversion. So, if you ask yourself, "How do I get to that peace?" then there is an answer—conversion. Conversion, in the first place, means to drop or leave all negative things, all distractions. The other meaning of conversion is to grow in love and peace and reconciliation.

A Christian life, of course, means that you should be able to do positive things. For that reason we can say that conversion will never finish, ever. Who of us can say my love is

40

complete? Who of us can say my peace is complete, my peace with God, and my peace with others? If we remain in our sin, our selfishness, and our pride, peace can never come. There you see the way to peace. So, we have to drop the negative things. We must begin to look at the positive things and we must do this without conditions.

We discover this thought with Jesus. He died on the cross for us without conditions. He didn't tell us: Would you please convert, and after that I shall love you. He died for us out of love, because He loved us without conditions.

Our Lady said to pray every day, The Creed and seven Our Father's, Hail Mary's, and Glory Be's. On the 14th of August, 1984, she said to pray the whole Rosary, the Joyful, Sorrowful and Glorious mysteries. She also invited us to fast two days of the week and she invited us to participate in Holy Mass daily, and go to confession once a month, and also to read the Bible. So you can see, she invites us to pray a lot. But the deep meaning of prayer here, is not to accummulate formulas of prayer during the day. The spirit of prayer and these messages is to begin to search for God.

There are people who pray, but they remain sinning. That means they have prayed because somebody said we must pray. But, if we begin to search for God, and if we begin to pray that way, our lives will actually change. Think about it.

Prayer in Our Lady's life was to always search for God, to be close to God. Be close to Jesus. Therefore, it is not so important how much we pray; but the most important thing is to search for the Lord, every day, in every situation, in prayer.

Perhaps we need to think about the Gospel, about the synagogue. We've said, "Oh, my Lord, I have fasted twice, I have prayed, I give money to the poor, but it was not accepted." Why? Because, as the Pharisee said, "I thank You Lord, that I am not like the one over there in the corner." That means he was praying and fasting in order to judge the others and that was a forbidden thing. So in praying and fasting, we must try to search for the Lord, search for the truth. We don't pray because others pray or others don't pray. We pray because we are searching for God, because we need God. I'm sure that you know there are many Christians who say, "Others don't pray or fast, so we don't need to pray and fast." We need to pray and fast without conditions. That is the spirit of prayer in the messages of Our Lady here.

For example, in the last message Our Lady said something very important for us. She said,

> *Don't look at others and don't slander them, but let your life be a testimony of the way to holiness.*

So, we must become positive, then we will live it. If you tell me it's not easy, or if you tell me it's impossible, let God be with you, because the Lord invites us to positive things. He wants to give us the strength to live in peace, reconciliations and holiness. In all simplicity, let's just be open before the Lord. Let the Lord be a gift to us. Our Lady said it's very urgent. Think about it.

As I said to you before, she invites us to fast. I know that there are many asking themselves, why fasting? It is a very secure fact that Our Lady invites us to fast one day a week. That used to be Friday. On the 14th of August, 1984, she added another day, Wednesday. And she said the idea would be to live with bread and water for the whole day. Why two days, why bread and water, why fast? I believe an important dimension with which to fast, is the Eucharistic dimension.

Jesus first spoke about the bread. And, afterwards, He did the miracle of the bread. On the third level, He gave His body as the bread. So we can see that Jesus tried to educate the disciples for this third level. For that reason, He spoke about the heavenly bread, and He multiplied the daily bread. Through living on bread two days a week we find it easier to discover Jesus in the bread. In the Eucharist, He is there, personally, with us and for us. Fasting is like a school for the Eucharist.

But there are other dimensions also. If you read the Bible you will discover that, through the prophets the Lord often invited the people to fast, and often to save them before some sort of bad situation. There are always three parts present:

Prayer, fasting and conversion. Our Lady is Queen of Prophets. So, for her, the same means are valid when she draws us to conversion, praying and fasting. Jesus did fasting; so did Our Lady and the Apostles. In the primitive Church, we find the two days of fast also. Then during the centuries that followed, we seemed to forget fasting, as you know. Now, our way is to fast two days a year, on Ash Wednesday and Good Friday. Our Lady wants us to do so every week. That is something very important for me. She wants this, very, very strongly. We really must fast, absolutely. Think about it.

The Madonna said that the messages come right from prayer. Our hearts are completely taken by material things. But through fasting, we receive a new freedom in our hearts; a freedom from material things, and an openness to prayer. You know Jesus' words: *Happy are those who are poor before the Lord.*

If you reflect on fasting, you must think of these words Jesus said. It doesn't mean we are supposed to have nothing. It means we should be open for God. We have often experienced that material things block us. We don't even see all the things that we have. We have become blind because we have so many material things. And if we don't see what we have, we want to have more and more. For that reason we have conflict in the families, and in the world. Conflicts and wars don't come because we are sharing our hearts, they come because we take things, want things, because of our pride.

If you begin to fast, you will begin to see how many things you have. You may also discover that you don't need most of them, and *that* for you is the beginning of a new peace. It is an opportunity to give and share with others.

It is sad, that as Christians, we are afraid to fast. We say in our prayers, that everywhere in the world we are brothers and sisters. But you know in this very moment there are people who are starving. These people are our brothers and sisters and they would be very happy to have that piece of bread to eat; and we are afraid to fast. Our Lady is the mother of all of us, and she wants us to understand that there are many other people in this world who need our help. Fasting is very important to our spiritual and physical well-being. I have had confirmation of this from many doctors—the value of fasting and self-discipline to our physical well-being. In any case, we should take that message of Our Lady seriously. You will also discover that it is not a danger to our lives. We can live, even if we fast.

Finally the message of faith. Here we have to discern belief and knowledge. There are many who say, "I believe," but really all they are saying is, "I know that there is a God." That's not enough. The Apostle St. James wrote, *The devil himself knows that God exists.* Many of those Christians who know there is a God, remain in sin, without any problem.

Here, the significance of faith is to abandon ourselves to God and let the will of God guide us. Decide for God! This is the faith of Our Lady. She let God guide her, even in her most difficult moments. She was totally abandoned to the Lord in every moment of her life, until the moment of Jesus' death, until He was put into the tomb, up until the moment of His Resurrection. Through it all, it was, *Thy will be done.* That is faith!

So put together all of the messages, but not just to have them. We need to begin to live them.

FR. SLAVKO BARBARIC, O.F.M.
St. James Parish, Medjugorje
May 11, 1988

Chapter 9

LET YOUR HEARTS BE NOT TROUBLED

Jesus spoke these words to His disciples when in a moment of uncertainty, they sensed that they would be left without Him. Brothers and sisters, these words provoke us to contemplate one of man's greatest problems and greatest fears; the uncertainty that man carries in his heart. For man and fear go together like clouds in the sky. There may be several clear days with not a cloud in the sky; then, suddenly the sky becomes blanketed with clouds and there's no blue sky left. Life's like that. Sometimes we feel sure of ourselves, fearless and brave, then along comes a moment of weakness. It was during a moment like this that Jesus said: *Let your hearts be not troubled.*

Moments of insecurity follow us from the cradle to the grave. It follows man his entire life. How many times have we been grateful to someone close to us, who has said the same thing Jesus said to His disciples, "Do not be afraid," particularly, when we knew that person would stand behind his words and was ready to give his all to protect us from that fear; as though he were to take us in his arms and carry us and share our fear, our helplessness?

The disciples knew such a moment. They sensed that

separation from Jesus was close at hand. They were faced with the difficult task that Jesus had left them with; but He gave them His word, *Do not be afraid. Let your hearts be not troubled. Believe in God and believe in Me.*

Jesus opened God's heart to us, and that's the light that shines on us, and only in that light, can we be secure. To find Jesus Christ, is to find God. That is why Jesus could say to His disciples, *Whosoever sees me, sees the Father.*

One of the greatest scholars of our century was once asked what his greatest discovery had been. "My greatest discovery," he said, "is the knowledge that I'm a sinner, and that Jesus Christ is my Saviour." The greatest discovery that man can make on this earth is this: "I'm a sinner, I'm lowly and wretched, but Jesus Christ is my Saviour." Jesus shows the way.

But, He went one step further. He told His followers that they were not alone. *I am the way,* said Jesus. No other words can express so beautifully the very essence of human life. Human life is a journey. Jesus came in human form along His own path. He took that path into the desert, where as a simple human being, He met His Heavenly Father. Jesus didn't try to escape from that path, in spite of all the temptations and difficulties He faced.

Later, the path led Him to His people and together, they embarked upon their journey through life. He raised up the powerless and the crippled. He forgave the desperate, strengthened those in need of His help, and healed the sick. That was His path, His way throughout life. His path finally led Him to Calvary; yet, Jesus didn't back down. He followed it to the end. When He called upon His disciples, He didn't ask them just to pray to Him. He said, *Follow Me.*

Of course, we must pray to Him, but Christians must make it their first priority to follow Jesus Christ. This is the clearest thing He said. Whenever He called upon one of His followers, He said, *Come, follow Me.* And to all He said, *Whosoever desires to follow me,* (that is, on his path through life) *He must carry his own cross.* We shouldn't look merely for what's beautiful and comfortable, but we must also accept the difficulties in life, as Jesus did, and follow along with Him.

Yes, Jesus is our "way." But as He also tells us, *I am the truth.* People say they live for the truth; but sometimes the truth means nothing more than our own selfish, often temporary, interests. This is what many people call "truth," and they are often ready to victimize others for their so-called truth. Jesus spoke of a different truth and He lived that truth. In fact, He endeavored to reveal the truth of life, the truth of God and man; and He served that truth. He was prepared to sacrifice His own life for it, and stood steadfast before Pilate and triumphed. Pilate was threatened by His defenselessness and began stammering in front of Jesus, Who bore no weapons or means of force. But, He possessed the truth He stood for, and for which He was ready to sacrifice His all.

Jesus also said, *I am the life.* Everyone says they love life, but today's man emphasizes the fact that he wants to live life to the fullest, that he wants to drink the cup of life to the last drop. Such a man is tranformed, in the end, into a destroyer of life. At no other time in history have so many unborn babies had their lives aborted, without ever having seen the light. There was never a time when the powerless were so despised. Why? Because mankind wants to live in luxury, to savor the cup of life to the last drop, whereas, Jesus was a servant of life.

I didn't come here to be served but to serve others.

Only those who are prepared to serve life obtain life, and are prepared to relinquish it. Those who pursue pleasures in life, leave devastation.

Brothers and sisters, what has been taking place for six years in this parish is that we've been traveling along a path; a path which isn't short and which one burst of enthusiasm won't satisfy. It's a path upon which we must all embark, but upon which we must also advance. Jesus foresaw this. Look at what Jesus left with us when He said, *I am the way.* First of all, He left His word that, as a community of believers, we wouldn't be alone along the way. And He taught us to love and to forgive everyone; for then the journey will be less difficult; life's burdens will be easier to bear. He left us His body to nourish us so we won't fall weakened and starving along the way. He left us the Sacrament of Reconciliation in case we should betray Him, stray from Him, overload ourselves with sin and can't go on alone anymore. Jesus took care of all that.

Today, it is appropriate that Our Lady calls us to peace. It's our primary goal, but it is also a gift. It is a gift that enables us to advance upon and ultimately reach, the final goal, which is the fullness of peace with God in eternity. Let me remind you that a quick burst of enthusiasm won't sustain us along the path we've embarked upon. Our Mother, Mary, is leading us to Jesus, Who provides us with all the resources to persevere in our pilgrimage; and we are not alone. May we never forget that.

Therefore, Medjugorje isn't some sort of passing fancy. Medjugorje doesn't exist simply to wet our human curiosity. Critical things are happening here for all humanity. We're called to a specific goal if we want peace within ourselves, and peace in our world. Peace can't exist without God, or without our conversion to God. It can't exist if we stray from the path. But, may we never forget we are not alone.

There are so many people who long for peace and search for it. Above all, our Saviour is with us; our Saviour Whom, one man says, is the greatest discovery of his life. "I am a sinner, but He is my Saviour Who helps me and gives me the ability to conquer my sinfulness and to triumph in glory with Him." He speaks the same words to us each day if only we care to listen.

> *Let your hearts be not troubled. Believe in God and believe in Me.* Amen.

FR. IVAN DUGANDZIC, O.F.M.
St. James Church, Medjugorje
May 17, 1988

Chapter 10

YOUR PILGRIMAGE, WHAT DOES IT MEAN?

There is a difference between a tourist and a pilgrim. A tourist is one who sightsees. A pilgrim is a prophet, one called by God, like Moses, to climb Mt. Sinai, meet God and free His people.

The other day I watched it raining. Some of the rain fell on the road and ran off into the gutter. Other drops fell into the river and went to the sea. Some disappeared in the earth. Some drops fell on roses in a garden and nourished them. Yet all the drops came from the same cloud. What happened depended on the place where they fell. So on your pilgrimage, some will get nothing out of it, some will receive pearls of love and peace and joy. It depends on you. But it is the same Medjugorje for all.

Our Lady has transformed Medjugorje. It speaks one language, the language of Our Lady. Medjugorje has become big. People from all nations have come to it. What the UN tried to do and could not, Our Lady has succeeded in doing in a short time. She has made of all nations, one family.

When the disciples went to Emmaus, Jesus went into their hearts and destroyed their short view of things. He opened up Moses and all the prophets to them, and showed how the

Messiah had to suffer to enter into glory. They all knew of Moses and the prophets; how come they did not know this? Why don't we?

What is Medjugorje really? I confess that I was one of the last to believe.

The first apparition occurred about two in the afternoon, Ivanka was the first to see Our Lady. Everybody knew her, for she had lost her mother just a month before. I was sad for her. She was like an orphan. She had been herding sheep, like the other children, when she saw a big light. She thought it was a fire on the hill, Podbrdo. The light was like a big wall. Mirjana was with her. They were afraid of this big light and both of them ran away. Then Ivanka turned back and looked again, and saw a lady, beckoning them with her hand to come to her. But they ran away. They ran into the village, saying they had seen Our Lady. Their parents were sad, and said it was blasphemy. The children repeated that they did see her. But they could not prove anything. The village was in turmoil. Everybody just waited for the next day.

So, the next day at the same time, 2:00 P.M., everyone came to the hill, and saw the light. All fell on their knees. Some in the thorns. The light vanished and the children saw Our Lady. So Vicka sprinkled holy water on her, and said: "If you are Satan, go away." Our Lady smiled, and said, *Do not be afraid.* They prayed with her, as Vicka's grandmother had told them, the Creed, seven Our Father's, seven Hail Mary's, and seven Gloria's.

Then Vicka turned around and said, "See, we didn't lie." Everybody believed, except the parents of the children, and me, Fr. Jozo.

Our Lady said to the children: *I have chosen you. I have called you. I need you. You are important to me.* She says those same words to every pilgrim.

Jakov was only a boy of ten, yet she had said to him, *You are important.* You can understand how Abraham was important, how Moses was. Centuries before Christ, Israel had a great crisis when Saul was king. A giant, Goliath, menaced the armies of Israel. What the king could not do, God could do. He found a boy, David. He said to him, "Do not be afraid. Go, in My name and meet Goliath." Later on, Christ said to the apostles, "Go in My name, heal the sick, raise the dead, drive out devils." And, in His name, they did just that. Likewise, armed in the name of the Lord, David slew Goliath and freed Israel.

David was important. He was important because he had been anointed by the Lord, and had become a prophet who could act in the name of the Lord. You too were anointed at Baptism and Confirmation. Not like warmongers, for God does not give us shot and shell, He gives us no other weapon but His name. The Church fought the Roman Empire for 300 years. Guess what? The one which had all the weapons lost the battle.

How will you overcome nations, the world, renew the Church? By writing a new book? No! By theologizing? No! Our Lady calls us to prayer. Because I know how to pray, I am a prophet. I am a prophet when I speak the word of God, and to God.

Jesus cannot be just a blur in our lives. He is the key, a sign, a sacrament. He gives signs to the Church and is a sign of the Church. There are many untruthful signs which many people follow. The saints never lost the sign. The Church cannot forget the saints. Israel cannot forget Moses. The Church cannot forget Jesus. Our Lady wants to show us Jesus, to give Him back to the people. You have to believe this, to have faith.

Jakov had said to me, "Tomorrow Our Lady will come into the Church."

I answered, "I cannot believe that. Yesterday she came on the hill, then the wineshop, then your house. I cannot believe that."

Jakov replied, "I cannot help you, because you have no faith." I confess to you now, I think about that.

In Nazareth, Jesus could do no works because of their

unbelief. I am very repentant and sad about my former doubts. Jakov was right. But I had great opportunity to make amends, through my time in prison when they sentenced me. Jakov was right. That night, at midnight, everyone went home, and waited.

The next day at noon, the church was packed. I saw this. Everybody was waiting for something, like people in a theater waiting for a show not yet begun. So, I said, "We will pray till 5:30." I gave instructions on the mysteries of the rosary and I was asking God to tell us the truth.

"I know You are on the altar," I said, "But I am not sure that Your Mother is on the hill."

At the 5:30 Mass, I told the people that we have the Mass, we don't need revelation. The people would not listen. They wanted witness. I could not give it.

The Bishop came and said the Mass, and gave support to the children. He said, "The children don't lie, they see Our Lady." The people applauded.

Jakov said that he had a message for us. Because he was so short, he asked to be put on the altar. There, he said that Our Lady wanted them to say the rosary. The people applauded again. "Pray the rosary every day, pray together. To pray the rosary, we can get to know Jesus." And so, it had happened.

Our Lady asks for prayer. Believe her, you are also important. The gift of prayer is waiting to be born in you. This is a gift of God. Just as spring touches all trees and causes them to bloom, so prayer is the spring of the Christian life. The body breathes when it is alive; when dead, it doesn't breathe. The soul breathes when it is praying. A Christian who prays is alive. A Christian who does not pray is dead.

Coming to Medjugorje is the spring of your Church. Become a blooming person. Bring a bouquet of flowers to America, be that bouquet, thus beautifying and converting your community.

She also asks us to fast. Not only not to eat; fasting is much deeper. It means to forgive, not to give our spouse the silent treatment; to renounce my plans that are contrary to theirs and militant against true happiness. It is to fast from words that destroy, that bring anger, fast from fashions, sports, etc.

The name of the idol is not important, we all have one. Destroy the idol. Fasting disposes us to do God's will. Our Lady said that Satan is powerful.

What does Our Lady want from Medjugorje? She wants us to find salvation through Jesus. And to find Jesus, through prayer, monthly confession, Scripture, Mass and fasting. All those things we know already. But we stopped. She is teaching us, again.

One day a lady from Vietnam came up to me and told me how it was when she was forced to leave her home during the war. Leaving her home, she turned and gave one last look. She saw the statue of Mary still sitting there. It seemed to say to her, "Don't leave me behind." She went back for it.

Don't leave Mary behind here in Medjugorje. Let her be mother of your family, of your parish, community, nation. Don't forget that the most important thing is to take Our Lady home with you.

She waited 6 years and 11 months for you to come here. She is patient. Be patient with yourself. Let the spirit grow in you gradually. But let it grow.

FR. JOZO ZOVKO
(A homily given May 24, 1988, at St. Elijah
Parish, Tihaljina, Yugoslavia. Fr. Jozo
was Pastor of St. James Church, in 1981).

Chapter 11

GOD WANTS TO MAKE YOU HOLY

The message begins with: *God wants to make you holy.*
Holiness is God's work in your hearts. He wants to make you holy. It is His activity. Mary invites us all to holiness. Her invitations are nothing new; but, do we accept?

Do you pray every day for the grace of holiness? If not, it could be because we do not understand that holiness is a grace, a gift of God Himself. We have to pray for this grace; and we must, because our holiness is good for others and for ourselves. For to be holy means to grow in love, in peace and in joy. To be holy is to be a good Christian. (Pause, and pray for holiness.)

Our Lady's message continues: *God wants to make you holy. And, therefore, through me, He is inviting you to complete surrender.*

What does complete surrender mean? It means, let go, let God. We say we know God, but do we really? We are invited to love, but do we? We are asked to forgive, do we? We know what we ought to do, but do we surrender? Who's in control of my life, God or me? My wants, my desires, my will, or His? (Pause, and pray for surrender.)

Next, Our Lady says: *Let Holy Mass be your life.* There

are two parts to the Mass. In the first part, Christ gives Himself to His Church; He surrenders Himself to us completely, to give us life and love. He wants to be our strength and life. In the second part, He sends us out to go and love people and surrender to them in love. The Eucharist means TO GIVE MYSELF TO GOD AND TO OTHERS IN LOVE. (Pause and pray and thank Mary for giving herself and her messages; and ask that Holy Mass be your life.)

Finally, she said: *Churches deserve respect and are set apart as holy because God, who became man, dwells in them day and night.*

There are four signs of respect in church.

- The first is silence in church. The church is not a place to have a social, nor even a musical recital.
- The second is attention. Keep your mind on the liturgy. What a reflection of in-attention when one is taking pictures during the Mass.
- The third is dress. Dress modestly when you come to this church. It is the house of God.
- The fourth is deportment. How do I make the sign of the cross? How do I genuflect? Respond to the prayers? And so on.

On television you can quickly know when two persons are friends. Can people discover from your actions in church, whether or not you are friends with Jesus? (Pause, for prayer, for reverence in church.)

FR. SLAVKO BARBARIC, O.F.M.
St. James, Medjugorje
May 25, 1988
(commentary on the message of April 25, 1988)

Chapter 12

WHY DO YOU COME HERE?

This is not an everyday experience. For many, it is not the first time. For others, it is a new and unique experience. So let us reflect on what the purpose of pilgrimage is and what it is meant to accomplish. Listen to your heart and mind, to what they are telling you. You can trust them.

A pilgrimage is a mirror to see yourself, not others (that would be a tour). Jesus spoke of pilgrimage when He said *...who has given up home, brothers or sisters, mother or father, children or property, for Me...and persecution besides...will receive everlasting life* (*Mk.* 10:29-30). You have left home and country, brothers and sisters, to come here. You have suffered persecution besides: plane delays, lost baggage, money spent.

By accepting these sacrifices, you allow yourself to learn that you have so many other brothers and sisters you did not know you had. You all become brothers and sisters, for you all share the same experiences and are all in the same boat.

Pilgrimage is like a school: you learn about yourself, the meaning and the purpose of your life.

The devil, however, wants to divert you from your purpose. The devil uses his power to urge us to build our kingdom

56

here on this earth. The message of Our Lady is the contrary; it is love, to learn to share with those in need.

Human sexuality is another gift of God to us. He created sex. And yet what has the devil done with it? He gets man to create pornography, dirty books, etc. How often the devil gets us to use our human gifts and possessions to further his work!

Human abilities and possibilities, gifts and talents, are all given us to create order and peace and beauty in the world. But the devil tries to turn the best into the worst. And sadly, we often let the devil possess these gifts of holiness. Humanly speaking, we cannot do anything about it. Mary does not offer us an escape. She tells us to be aware of the devil and to pray. Our Lady's plan is simple: pray! God will do the rest.

Pray that God brings order into your lives. We do not have to think too much, to run around too much. We need simply to pray. Pray daily. Pray the way you know how. Pray that God helps you not to make the wrong moves, not to let the devil use your powers and abilities to further his own ends.

Prayer is a courageous thing to do. It is not easy. It is not compatible with our contemporary thinking, for prayer does not earn money, it does not entertain, it does not offer rest and recreation. Prayer does not make sense to the world. It is just the opposite of the world. Our Lady does not ask you to be perfect in prayer. It is not full of high experiences. She just says, "Pray." Take the rosary every day. Go to your neighbor. Be a good neighbor.

Our pilgrimage is a mirror to see ourselves—a courageous search for our soul. It is a look into our past. Recall the last five years of your life; the places where you have been. Look at your check stubs and see what you spent your money on. Am I comfortable with all this? Am I happy with what I have done? Was it a way to happiness?

You are not here to see the seers or sights. You are here as pilgrims, to search for God, to see Him face to face, that He may take your hand and lead you day by day.

God will give each one at Medjugorje the experience he

needs. So many come hoping to find peace. Yet, some meet people who are unkind and thoughtless, bathrooms that are not at all up to expectations, and so on. We must not look to the things outside us, but to the heart within us. The problems are not outside us, but inside us. Look to your heart; do not be a reactor!

You are called to conversion here. At first it is exciting, joyful, like falling in love. But then the honeymoon is over. Conversion is like driving a car because every turn is a temptation and every oncoming car is a danger. Therefore, you must be alert. Drive carefully, for the devil seeks to smash you up. Drive constantly, prayerfully, for you must go on.

A danger on the road you must watch out for is getting over-tired. We are vulnerable when we are tired. We stop praying when we are tired. We let activities and money take over. That is why you will find resting places on the roadside. Come and rest with me awhile. A pilgrimage, a retreat—these are necessary for the journey.

People come two or three times to Medjugorje. Each time they must get new graces. If you buy a pair of pants for a child, it won't fit him a year later. He grows. So you must search for deeper meaning and growth each time you visit Medjugorje. In marriage, one grows in the knowledge and acceptance of each other. Similarly, we must grow in heart and mind. God does not allow us to stay in the same place.

What should you do for Medjugorje?

Nothing, but be holy. That is the best we can do. God is calling us to this. He needs us all for Himself. Seek out the reasons, in your mind, why you came here.

SVETOZAR KRALJEVIC, O.F.M.
St. James Parish, Medjugorje
May 27, 1988

PART II

INTRODUCTION

Chapter 13

IN APPRECIATION

Over 12 million people have gone to Medjugorje. They come from all over the world. Over one million confessions have been heard there. In this day and age, that's amazing. That's a gift from God, and a gift to Our Lady.

An increasing percentage of pilgrims to Medjugorje, are from North America. The English language has become the predominate foreign language there. Providing spiritual direction for these pilgrims, have been hundreds of American Priests, and accompanied by hundreds of nuns and other religious.

To them, we offer our sincere thanks. We applaud their commitment. We recognize that commitment, to their vocations, to Jesus Christ, to His Church, to His Pope, and to His Mother. We applaud their commitment to God's people.

It does not come down to whether they, "believe in the apparitions." It comes down to their belief in the messages, the conversions, the faith, the reaffirmation of the Gospel truths that Medjugorje conveys. It comes down to their commitment to extend their ministry to thousands and thousands of people, who are making a special pilgrimage, seeking spiritual fulfillment.

Many of them have something special to say about Medjugorje. Many of these priests have come to find that the Mother of Jesus has now taken up a special place in their lives. Alleluia!

We cannot print all the words from all of them. But we bring you a few on the following pages. On behalf of all those inspired by these words, and to all those in religious life who make up this growing Army of Our Lady, and to those who have willingly and openly expressed their thoughts throughout the remainder of this book, "Our Thanks!"

Bill Reck
The Riehle Foundation

Chapter 14

"AM I NOT HERE WHO AM YOUR MOTHER?"

We have been told by Fr. Slavko Barbaric that the main message of Medjugorje is the presence of Our Lady. This is the same message she gave to Juan Diego on the hill of Tepyac near Mexico City on Dec. 12, 1521:

Am I not here who am your Mother.... Am I not your fountain of joy.... Is there anything else you need?

Mary is with us; her presence is within us; she is near to us, especially when we pray. At the beginning of our prayer we should ask her to be with us, to pray with us, and to teach us how to pray with our hearts. To recognize her presence, we need to look within ourselves as she has reminded us: "Why are you so reluctant to open your hearts? What does it take to convince you? Why is it that you must see to believe? I tell you look within and you shall see."

So often—too often—we become distracted by signs or by our desire to see something with our eyes, instead of "seeing" with our hearts. Our journey back to Jesus is one of the heart. It is a pilgrimage of prayer, which will consume the rest of our days here on earth. If we allow Our Lady to lead us, if we call upon her to be with us, then our journey, our pilgrimage, will not be directionless. We will not wander because she will be our guide.

To grasp the fact, as the visionary Vicka reiterated in June, 1988, that when we pray "Our Lady hears you just like she hears me," is very important. It is really essential to understand this so that we can begin journeying on the path of a deeper spirituality—toward a closer relationship with Jesus. As we present our prayers with her to Jesus, Our Lady will help us give all to Him, all of who we are. She will help us turn over to Him, in prayer, everything—even our sins—so that we can be healed. He wants to fill us with His joy, so that our joy may be complete.

To live the messages of Our Lady, which we have received and are continuing to receive, we need to pray. Prayer must now be a priority in our lives. Only in prayer, and through prayer, can we truly live out her messages. Only in prayer, and through prayer, will we come to the undeniable conviction that Jesus is *real*, and that He has allowed His Mother to be with us in a most effective and real way, not only in Medjugorje, but in our hearts.

The main message for us, for each of us, too, is that Our Lady is with us. She wants to give us her motherly direction; she wants to speak to us words of comfort and encouragement and challenge. She offers us the invitation to peace. But, notice, it's only an invitation. We need to go to her more earnestly in our prayer. We need to be more dedicated to prayer in our daily routine. We need to go to her, place ourselves in her arms, in her mantle, so that she can lead us to Jesus. Accept that invitation.

Read, again, her words spoken to Juan Diego on the hill of Tepyac. Let them now, again in our day, penetrate our hearts, and take root in our very being. She is the same Lady who is speaking in Medjugorje. She is our Mother. She is with us. Look within and you will meet her, and she will lead you to her Son.

I am your merciful Mother, the Mother of all who love me, of those who cry to me, of those who have confidence in me....Am I not here who am your Mother? Are you not under my shadow and protection? Am I not your fountain of joy? Are you not in the folds of my mantle? In the crossing of my arms? Is there anything else you need?

FR. JACK SPAULDING
St. Maria Goretti Parish
Scottsdale, Arizona

(Fr. Spaulding and Fr. Dale Fushek, through their LIFE TEEN Ministry, produced a film on Medjugorje, for teenagers. It is available from Epoch Universal Publications Inc. Phoenix, AZ.)

The statue in St. James Church.

Chapter 15

THE
CROSS AND
MEDJUGORJE

The plain of Medjugorje is surrounded by beautiful hills and mountains. That is how it got its name: "Mid Hills," between the mountains. Two mountains now dominate the area; the hill of the cross and the hill of the apparitions.

The hill of the cross, Krizevac, is so called because in the Holy Year of 1933, the 19th centenary of Redemption, the villagers built a 40-ft. concrete cross on its summit. Only when one sees the treacherously steep, rocky paths these people had to climb to carry all the necessary materials, does one appreciate their sacrificial faith. Our Lady is reported to have said that the providence of God took that cross into account. On the Feast of the Exaltation of the Cross, September 14th, vast crowds have gathered each year there for the celebration of Mass.

Facing the hill of the cross, on the left, is the smaller hill of the original apparitions, (Podbrdo). There, too, the paths are steep and incredibly rocky. But the view is awe-inspiring, as one feels that he is on Mt. Nebo and, like Moses, is allowed to look into the Promised Land. Below is the plain with the twin-spired Church of St. James, surrounded by the vineyards, wheat and tobacco fields of the farmers.

Although it is Our Lady's apparitions that made Medjugorje famous, what dominates the area is the presence of the cross. There is that gigantic concrete cross overlooking the plain. But also, and strangely, the sites of the original apparitions on Podbrdo are marked by multiple smaller crosses.

Mary identified herself to the six young visionaries at Medjugorje as the Queen of Peace. In view of these two presences, it recalls what St. Paul told the Colossians, (*Col.* 1:20): *Christ made peace through the blood of His Cross.*

As the cross is very much a part of the landscape of Medjugorje, so is it also a characteristic of its spirituality. Sacramental life abounds as dozens of priests console repentant sinners with absolution; these same priests then distribute Holy Communion to the overflowing crowds at the Masses. The graces of these sacraments flow from the sacrifice of the Cross.

These farmers, with their simple lifestyle, probably envied the rest of the world, with all of its luxuries. Now, that world flies to Medjugorje for that elusive element that the luxurious world cannot give: Peace! From the biblical perspective, that is obviously what St. Paul speaks about in 1 Cor. 1:27:

> *God chose those whom the world considers absurd to shame the wise; he singled out the weak of this world to shame the strong. He chose the lowborn and despised, those who count for nothing to reduce to nothing those who are something; so that mankind can do no boasting before God.*

Can a practical spirituality be formulated from the events at Medjugorje? That should not be too difficult, since the message revolves around peace. We want permanent peace; not here one day and gone the next. And since Jesus *made peace through the blood of His Cross,* (*Col.* 1:20) the way to peace for us is the same royal way of Jesus—the cross. Since we want daily peace, it must come through our daily cross. Jesus said, *Pick up your cross daily and come follow Me.* (*Lk.* 9:23). If we learn to live with, then to accept, and finally love our cross, then we shall develop that peace of Christ.

What does a cross consist of? Two beams—vertical and horizontal. Our relationship to God is frequently described as a vertical relationship, from earth to Heaven above, while our relationship to other human beings is described as horizontal, on an equal level. Thus our relationships constitute the matter of our cross; the vertical and horizontal relationships of life.

Our vertical relationship with God consists of our duties toward God. This can be summarized in the term "worship," to give God His due, a loving service for the praise of God. Crossing the vertical is the horizontal—our duties toward others. This can be summarized in the term "witness."

So our daily cross is thus composed of our duties and responsibilities toward God and others, in the form of worship and witness to the Gospel in our daily living. The better we fulfill these requirements daily, the better we carry our cross daily, and achieve our Christian peace daily.

Today, there are some who stress the elimination of all suffering through healing. But some have a vocation to suffering. And Mary's children are numbered among them. At Fatima, she asked the children if they would accept the suffering God allowed in their lives, for the conversion of sinners. Besides the great moral suffering of misunderstanding and doubt, Jacinta and Francesco were victims of the international influenza epidemic. Jacinta, aged 9, had to undergo an operation, and died alone, separated from family and friends. St. Maximilian Kolbe, the knight of the Immaculata, volunteered to replace a fellow prisoner, offering his life at the death camp at Auschwitz. The list is long.

So, Mary allows a sword to pierce the hearts of some of her children so that they may have perfect spiritual resemblance and identity with her—at the foot of the Cross. Mary helped pay the price of that peace, "made through the blood of His Cross." So, too, if we stand with Mary daily, then she will help us fulfill our duties to God and neighbor through our daily worship and witness, forming the vertical and horizontal beams of our daily cross.

Medjugorje places us mid-hills, between the hill of the Cross and the hill of her presence through the apparitions. She unites us to both, that we may have the effect of both, Peace! As we achieve our personal peace daily, so we can then share that gift with others.

FR. STANLEY SMOLENSKI
St. Martha Parish
Enfield, CT

(part of an article by Fr. Smolenski in QUEEN of all hearts Magazine, Nov.-Dec. 1987.)

Chapter 16

MEDJUGORJE: AN EDUCATION IN INNER-HEALING AND PRAYER GROUPS

People frequently ask me what I think of Medjugorje. My bottom line response goes back to a question which I have often asked myself. What would it be like if an entire parish or town really believed in Jesus? We can imagine what it must have been like in the very early Church as we read about the community of believers in "The Acts of the Apostles." But I haven't seen anything like that in my day. When I first stepped off the bus in front of the Church of St. James, in Medjugorje, and walked up to be with the people in front of the overcrowded church attending the evening Croatian Mass, I knew the answer to my question. Here I found a people who radiated in the way they live, that they truly believe in Jesus, for they live His way of love.

They maintain this daily conversion through a great return to Church, gathering each evening for three hours of prayer, rosary, Eucharist, homily, healing prayers and adoration. They fast on bread and water and empty themselves to God. Before the first Sunday of the month they pray and fast for three days and go to the Sacrament of Reconciliation, and then seek reconciliation in their families at a reconciliation dinner on Sunday. Jesus' Gospel of love and reconciliation is apparent in the lives of the people of Medjugorje.

For me, like many others, Medjugorje has also become an education. There, Vicka, one of the seers, offers her life and her illness to the world, for souls. Vicka's suffering is well-known, but we need to see the lesson in it, as she does. It has focused me personally in my ministry, in a whole different direction. God does many physical healings, as He did in the Gospels, but they are signs and means of attracting us to His real message. And once He's attracted us to the message of the healing of the heart—forgiveness, reconciliation, getting out of our sinful ways, then we are like the cripple who was let down on the mat before Him in the crowd, and He said, *Your sins are forgiven you.* But because people disbelieved, He said as well, that the man should get up, pick up his mat and walk. That was to be a sign that the main healing of forgiving his sins was what He had really granted, and why Jesus comes to us.

This is what Vicka is teaching me; that there are real healings, but they are also signs. In Medjugorje there are over 300 physical healings on record in the parish that seem to be miraculous or cannot be easily explained by doctors. But what is happening in far greater numbers, is that there are tens of thousands whose lives have been converted, who have found Jesus. That's the miracle of Medjugorje, the conversion of lives. Certainly it's the miracle I've experienced.

Therefore, what I'm beginning to find, is that in praying for healing, I often no longer really know what to pray for and many times in my own heart, I am more comfortable just to pray in tongues, and let the Lord do what He wants. But I do know that He wants healing on the internal level, whether He gives a physical healing or not. That we can be sure of; that's where His graces really count. Vicka has shown me that. For somebody to be healed in heart, to offer joyfully, their burdens, all burdens, what a difference and what a power that is. Being a witness to other people; the energy that comes from that.

Vicka has taught me that. She is vibrant. She is the most joyful person in Medjugorje. She will talk with pilgrims incessantly, even though she should be in bed with her illness.

The prayer groups in Medjugorje greatly impress people, as they have me. They were basically started through the two young locutionists, Jelena and Marijana. Jelena prayed every day, for over a year, for the gift of talking with Mary, and then suddenly one day, Mary spoke to Jelena in her heart. Those two along with about seven other young girls, started the first prayer group there. They just prayed, constantly, and they still meet.

In 1983, Mary invited them to invite the young people in the parish, to give four years of their life to a prayer group formation, with these requirements: minimum of three hours per day of prayer, and that they make no other life commitments during that time. It was like a novitiate, a time for Mary to form them. Over fifty young people responded to the four year commitment.

They meet in prayer sessions three times a week. Mary directed them in their prayer, through Jelena. They meet for 1-1/2 to 2 hours. Often they meet early in the mornings, like 6:30 A.M. They have prayers of praise, they pray the rosary, read the Scriptures of the day, the readings of the Mass. They reflect and meditate on those. They have intercessory prayer, quiet meditation, faith sharing of God's presence in their lives. They have song interwoven throughout.

There is no "one way" to have a prayer group. Mary has asked that every parish have a prayer group, and that all people give at least one hour to God every day. The prayer groups are not charismatic any more than the apparitions are charismatic. She has not asked for charismatic prayer groups as it is understood in the States, but in the sense of the Holy Spirit being present wherever people are gathered in prayer. They do not usually use in their prayer groups, the external signs that are associated with the Charismatic Renewal in North America, but prayer to and for the gifts of The Holy Spirit is present. Prayer is the heart of what Mary is inviting, and she wants families and groups to come together to pray, and to use all forms of prayer.

They use a lot of music there, but differently. I'm drawn to it. It is always a call to quietness, to quiet prayer. There is another strong prayer group called "Our Lady's Prayer Group." This is a group of slightly older youth, headed up by Ivan and Maria, a smaller group of approximately twelve people. They often meet after the three hour service in the church, and go up the mountain to pray another couple of hours at night. They have a pattern, a rhythm, of both music and quiet time. They sing traditional hymns, move into prayer, an Our Father, a Hail Mary, then quiet. When the Spirit moves again, another song.

They try to say something special in that pattern, and I found that very much drawing me, and many of my pilgrims, into prayer. I could also see the struggle some of my American brothers and sisters were having with silence. It is something spiritual directors have to deal with, helping people respect the uncomfortable aspect of silence in the beginning, so that they can listen on a deeper level. The group would pray a rosary, but always with songs after each decade. Hymns and meditations are a part of their rosary.

Medjugorje is a place of prayer, and the urgency Mary seeks there is to bring people into prayer. Secondly, is the fasting invitation as a means of emptying ourselves, and opening ourselves to a greater simplicity and to welcome the Lord within us. They add up to conversion, to reconciliation. Jesus lived in total unity with the Father, while on earth. How did Jesus achieve it? With prayer and fasting. As you read the Scriptures, what is the power in both the New and Old Testament? It is prayer and fasting linked. There is the power.

Medjugorje is an education. How are we to come to know Jesus, except by being around Him, or by listening to the call of His Mother? A relationship with Jesus. If I'm going to open up to Jesus, I've discovered I have to let go of things within me; and I've discovered there's many things I couldn't do, and that is where prayer and fasting fit in. I'm beginning to see fasting as simply, "I can't fill my cup with God if it's already filled with Father Al." I have to empty it of Al, and you first have to find a way to do that. It's frustrating to try to empty oneself of everything that is selfish, because we give more priority to our sinfulness by focusing on it. I found that what was more important is the question; "Can I simply make an offering of myself?" And that's when fasting came. It led to being able to let go of other distracting things as well—like television. We need to be able to let go of anything that can become a pattern that dominates us. Ultimately, Mary's fasting is to lead to fasting from sin.

Prayer and fasting, those two go together. Fasting is not done alone, it is a time of prayer, it is the attraction to prayer.

At the beginning of Mary's weekly Thursday messages, she invited:

> *Dear Children, in this parish, start converting yourselves. In that way all those who come here will be able to convert.*

It is true. Millions have come, and many return home with a new zeal for prayer and fasting and their lives begin to change, to be converted. I know it is happening to me, and I see it in others. Mary's love at Medjugorje is so much a part and call within my life that I can no longer conceive what my life would be like without Mary, Queen of Peace, at Medjugorje. Yes I am convinced that this is of God and that I cannot afford not to hear and live, the Gospel message here.

FR. ALFRED WINSHMAN, S.J.
Loyola House
Boston, MA

(Part of an address at
The Catholic Charismatic Renewal,
March, 1988, Alberta, Canada.)

Chapter 17

THE SPIRIT OF MEDJUGORJE

It was in the fall of 1985, when I first heard about the Blessed Virgin Mary's appearance in Medjugorje, Yugoslavia. Since then, the news of these apparitions has circulated throughout the world and people have been coming from virtually every continent, in ever-increasing numbers.

These reported apparitions at Medjugorje have not yet received explicit approval by the Church, but this is not unusual, because the Church always proceeds cautiously in such matters. But when Pope John Paul II was asked if people could go to Medjugorje, he reportedly said: "Ah, Medjugorje! If they pray and do penance when they go there, let them go, let them go." During the past year I learned of many priests who had gone there as spiritual directors to the faithful, on private pilgrimages. Soon I found myself really longing for the opportunity.

It happened on April 8, 1988. Apparently it was the Lord's will that I make this pilgrimage, because I was able to purchase my passport and visa very quickly, and everything else seemed to just fall into place for me to make the trip. We arrived in the village on Sunday, April 10th, at 3:30 P.M. and after getting settled in our homes in the village, it was still

74

in time to go to church for the three hour service that occurs every day from 6:00 to 9:00 P.M.

Literally every inch of space in St. James Church was packed with local village people and pilgrims from all over the world. What a powerful phenomenon this was in itself. I was deeply touched by the atmosphere of faith, peace, prayer, and inner conversion of peoples' lives that I experienced there.

I personally experienced the inner conversion of peoples' hearts in the Sacrament of Reconciliation, as I heard confessions several hours each day; conversions of people who had been away from the church, 5, 10, 20 years or more, as well as those who had been going to church, but were moved by the grace of God to make a beautiful Confession.

Other occasions of special grace for me were the continual prayer pilgrimages on rugged, rocky paths to the top of Apparition Hill and Cross Mountain, located on either side of Medjugorje; the large crowds of people attending Mass in various languages throughout the day, and the continual stream of people in and out of St. James Church to spend time in prayer.

Probably the peak moment of my time there occurred the first day, when I arrived at the cross on Apparition Hill, which marks the spot where Mary first appeared to the visionaries in June, 1981. I seemed to sense a special presence of Mary and Jesus at that moment, so I just knelt there in prayer for some time before continuing on my pilgrimage. From my experience at Medjugorje, I feel called to more intense prayer and weekly fasting.

What the visionaries are saying is very simple: "We have seen the Madonna, the Mother of God, the Gospa," (as they say in Croation.) At first Fr. Jozo Zovko, the pastor at that time, was baffled and fearful and negative, but through his own conversion he decided that the hand of God was evident and the events were genuine. At his direction, the stream of pilgrims was channeled into the Church, where long prayers, the Eucharist and powerful preaching stressed conversion, peace, and prayer. This continues to be a daily experience for people who come to St. James, a journey which started seven years ago.

Meanwhile, life goes on in Medjugorje. Our Lady appears daily, and she still gives messages for the whole world on the 25th of each month. People still fast and pray on the mountains. Healings and conversions are daily occurrences. The Rosary and Mass are said in many languages, and it isn't unusual to see 50 or 60 priests concelebrating Mass on an ordinary day. The lines to confession grow longer, and lives are being changed. Pilgrims who go there, are transformed into people who live their faith openly, and who bear witness to it in a vital way.

All that is taking place in St. James Parish in Medjugorje is being watched throughout the world. Personally, I believe the messages and events occurring there are very authentic, because they coincide so well with the Gospel message. It remains to the Holy Spirit to verify this.

FR. DUAINE COTE
Our Lady of Peace Church
Mayville, North Dakota

Chapter 18

ACCEPT
AND USE
THE GIFTS

At Mass today, we heard a Gospel we have heard many times:

Ask and you will receive, knock and it will be opened, seek and you will find.

But the problem is, we ask but we don't wait to receive. We knock and don't wait for it to be opened. We seek but we don't wait to find. We want God to do our will. We say, "Thy will be done, but God, here's my plan, give it Your blessing." We always want God to fit our time schedule, don't we. Life is waiting, but waiting according to God's plan, to do God's will.

This morning, again, He has said to us, *Ask and you will receive.* He says the one who asks WILL receive. Now this is the word of God. God is not kidding. He is not lying. He says if you ask, you will receive. This is the word of God. God's word is creative, and what God says happens. And He says to us today, "If you ask Me, you will receive. If you look for Me, you will find Me."

So, now all of us are here on a pilgrimage. What are we going to ask God for? I would like to make two suggestions,

77

two gifts. And if, in faith, we ask Him, He said He would give it to us. God will give the gift, BUT, we have to accept it, and we have to use it. So, what two gifts does a pilgrimage to Medjugorje suggest? What are we going to bring home with us from here, from this place of apparitions?

I would suggest that we ask for two gifts: First, that we ask God for the gift of full conversion of life; and second, the gift of prayer. If we ask God, He will give them to us.

Somehow, this spells out for me what Medjugorje is really all about; the gift of full conversion, not playing games with God, going to Church Sunday morning and then forgetting Him the rest of the week. Jesus said, *I've come to give you life,* not to play games.

Full conversion! What is this conversion, this repentance that we talk about all week? It is making a U-turn; because every day we tend to go off the road because of our human weakness, because of all the distractions around us. So the gift of full conversion is the gift of a U-turn in our life; a "gift" because we cannot do it ourselves, we are too weak. We need His Spirit. A converted life is a life of living for Jesus Christ. That is what our faith is all about. It is not a head trip by which we know certain dogma. It's living it; living for Jesus Christ.

To be converted to God means we cannot go along with the world in which we are living. Let's face it. We live at a time and in a world that has abandoned Jesus Christ. I'm afraid there are too many Christians who live not in the world, but for the world, playing games with God. Conversion is what Mary teaches here, to us, to her children.

Therefore, a life of full conversion means that we be different. To be a Christian, means to be different, that you don't go along with the world, but you stand up for Jesus Christ and His Gospel, and His Church.

But we don't always like to be different, do we? People will make fun of us. That's Satan's move. That's the sacrifice of Medjugorje, a life of conversion, of faith, living for God and standing up for what you believe. It's making a choice for

Jesus Christ, and not the times in which we're living. That hurts; that's the sacrifice. We don't like to fast. That hurts; that's the sacrifice. *That's Gospel.* That is the first gift—full conversion.

The second gift is the gift of prayer. But whoever receives the gift, must accept, and use it.

We speak of saying prayers, and many times that is all we do; we "say prayers." Hear Mass! Say the rosary! We have to go beyond the saying. It's like turning on the tape recorder, let it say the rosary. Prayer at Medjugorje, Mary says, must be from the heart. It's not so much saying, as communicating with God, the praying of the heart.

Mary tells us that the greatest prayer is the Mass, specifically, the Eucharist. Eucharist is really the last prayer of Jesus Christ, sacramentalized. His sacrifice becomes present, and we offer ourselves, "with Him, through Him, and in Him." It's a prayer of Christ, and our prayer, joined together. For Mass is not only the sacrifice of Christ, present in a Sacrament, it's a sacrifice of the Church through, and in, Jesus Christ.

Prayer is a gift. We must accept it and use it. That means we must take the time—not only on Sunday morning. Prayer is food and drink for our souls. We eat every day. We must pray every day. Take the time to be with your God. The gift of prayer will be given if we ask.

Jesus invited Peter to get out of the boat and walk on the water. He didn't lift him out of the boat. Peter had to do it. He received the gift but he had to do his part.

Let us ask God for the gift of full conversion, making religion our life, not a game. Seek the gift of prayer, for those who learn to pray, those who learn to love, are those who live in peace. That is what Medjugorje does. It makes the word of God so concrete. It puts flesh on it. This town is so down to earth, where the Mother of God appears. Religion is not pie in the sky here. "I am as close to you," God says, "as the very air you breathe." Medjugorje is life, is that breath. It's real, and in Him we move, and have our life. Let us pray for each other as we pray for these gifts.

God says, "Ask me, I will give them to you. Will you accept them, and will you use them?" If we do, our life will change. If you go home the same as you came, then you missed the word that Medjugorje brings. Through Mary's intercession, let the Lord change us. Use the gifts.

FR. AUGUSTINE DONEGAN, T.O.R.
Franciscan Univ. of Steubenville
(homily at the English Mass, in Medjugorje, Feb. 25, 1988)

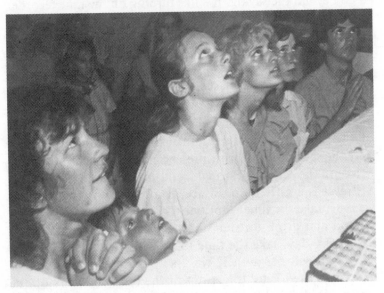

Vicka, Jakov, Ivanka, Mirjana, Maria, Ivan.

Chapter 19

THE REAL
SECRET OF
MEDJUGORJE

It did not occur to me until I arrived in Medjugorje that the Feast of the Annunciation would fall during the week of my stay. The date of the feast, March 25, also coincided with one of our Our Lady's public messages. Since January 8, 1987, a special message is given by Our Lady on the 25th of each month. Previously, these public messages had come every Thursday, beginning with March 1, 1984. Over 150 of them are in print.

The Annunciation Day message came, as usual, through the visionary Maria, who was in Italy on an extended prayer retreat with others from her prayer group. She received the message during her apparition that day. After the apparition, Maria wrote down the Croatian words and read them over the telephone to Father Slavko in Medjugorje. The message was immediately translated into other languages and then posted at St. James Church and relayed to various Medjugorje centers around the world. Father Philip Pavich translated the message into English.

The Message of March 25, 1988, reads:

Dear children! Today also I am inviting you to

a complete surrender to God. You, dear children, are not conscious of how God loves you with such a great love. Because of it, He permits me to be with you so I can instruct you and help you find the way of peace. That way, however, you cannot discover if you do not pray. Therefore, dear children, forsake everything and consecrate your time to God and then God will bestow gifts upon you and bless you.

Little children, do not forget that your life is fleeting like the spring flower which today is wondrously beautiful, but tomorrow has vanished. Therefore, pray in such a way that your prayer, your surrender to God, may become like a road sign. That way your witness will not only have value for yourselves, but for all of eternity. Thank you for having responded to my call.

In the beginning of this report, I said that I saw no signs or wonders in Medjugorje. Yet, I must confess, that as I read over the above message on March 27, Palm Sunday, I experienced a deep peace and, sinner though I am, a deep sense of God's unconditional love and that of Our Lady.

It was a sunny morning and I was sitting on a rock behind the Church of St. James. In those words, I felt some of the "great love" to which Mary is leading us. The message of "complete surrender" seemed so perfect for the feast of Mary's Annunciation.

To me, at the heart of the Medjugorje message is this: The source of the world's healing is first of all God's burning love. It is a loving God who brings about the world's salvation and not simply our efforts, important as they are as instruments of God's saving will. Only through surrender to God (prayer) can the branch be in living union with the vine and able to bear fruit. The good news out of Medjugorje is the same as the Good News out of Judea: A saving God is with us and invites us to respond.

Mary's messages always end with the words: *Thank you for having responded to my call.* Her own "complete surrender" to God's overflowing love reminds us that she knows much about "responding." If God's "great love" seeking our response is the secret of Medjugorje—and I believe it is—then the world can only be blessed when it accepts this good news.

FR. JACK WINTZ, O.F.M.
Cincinnati, OH

(Fr. Jack Wintz is the associate editor of the St. Anthony Messenger Magazine, and has written a very comprehensive article in that publication, of which the above is a summary.)

St. Anthony Messenger
1615 Republic St.
Cincinnati, OH 45210

Chapter 20

A YEAR
OF
GRACE

This past year has been a very exciting one for me. In a period of 12 months, I have had the opportunity to go to Medjugorje, help host the visit of the Pope to Phoenix, spend a day and a half with Mother Teresa of Calcutta, have Mother Angelica visit our parish for a weekend, and go to the Basilica of Our Lady of Guadalupe.

When I think about it, it "boggles" my mind. And in some ways, it also scares me. I know that God has set these events in my life for a purpose. Maybe it's to teach me something, maybe it's to set me up for something, or maybe it's because I'm hard headed and am a slow learner. But, I do know one thing for sure, He has caught my attention.

The wonderful chain of events started with our trip to Medjugorje. We went there as part of the LIFE TEEN program to tape a television show for teenagers. The experience, personally, was incredible. I have always had a love for Mary, and I've always held her fondly in my heart. But, something changed during our trip. My love for her moved beyond being sentimental, to becoming a relationship with a PERSON. The apparitions said to me, loud and clear, that the Blessed Mother is not a plastic statue that we should have respect for. The

Madonna, the Lady, is a woman, who shares in the eternal life of her Son, and who God uses to bring the presence of the Son into the world. Mary is real! The apparitions proved to me, and hopefully to all of us, that her unique role in salvation history is STILL present in the mind of the Father, and that He continues to use her.

As the year has progressed, I began to learn another very powerful lesson. The "HOLIEST" people in the world (not just my world, the WHOLE world), all have a close and intimate love and relationship with Mary. The visionaries, of course, have that kind of relationship, but so does the Holy Father. Mother Angelica (EWTN) devotes herself to the Eucharist and to the Mother. Mother Teresa walks with a rosary in her hand (one blessed in Medjugorje by the Blessed Mother).

All three of these saintly people are deeply committed to the Blessed Mother. And, I had the opportunity to ask Mother Angelica and Mother Teresa if they believed the Blessed Mother was appearing to the children. Both, without hesitation, believe.

The trip to Guadalupe only deepened my new insights of a deeply personal relationship with Mary. Living in the southwest, I knew the story of Guadalupe. What I did not know, was what the people of Mexico believed about the Blessed Mother.

They do not believe she simply appeared four centuries ago, they believe that the image is really her presence. They believe that they simply come to see their Mother, the Mother of the Saviour. I was surprised, too, to see how deeply the people coming to the Basilica in Mexico, believe in the apparitions in Medjugorje. The people of Mexico came for a special celebration of the anniversary of the apparitions in Yugoslavia (June 25). They know, it is the same WOMAN!

The Father is using Mary in my life to deepen my ability to love, and to deepen my commitment to Christ. In the past year, my love for the Mass and for the Eucharist has deepened. My love for the poor has grown. My desire for prayer and to abandon myself is changing. These are gifts that Our Lady is giving to me. She is not "distracting" me from God, from the Son, but she is enlivening my heart with Their love.

God is using Mary for us all. In His mercy, He is sending her into our world to call us to prayer, fasting, and conversion. Through her, and through her love, His love is flowing into our hearts. There is no doubt in my mind, in my heart, or in my soul that the apparitions are real! And, there is no doubt in my mind, that God is using Mary for me, for us, to call us to holiness. We must be open to experience this call, and we MUST listen to the message. It is not her message, she is but a vessel bringing the WORD into the WORLD.

I do not know how any year can top this past year for me. But I do know, that the real growth in me is just beginning, and that God, is using our Mother to help me to be a better priest, a better Christian, a better person.

FR. DALE J. FUSHEK
Vicar of Worship, Diocese of Phoenix
Pastor, St. Timothy's, Mesa, Arizona

(Fr. Fushek and Fr. Jack Spaulding, through their LIFE TEEN Ministry, produced a film on Medjugorje, for teenagers. It is available from Epoch Universal Publications Inc., Phoenix, AZ).

Chapter 21

MEDJUGORJE:
A RETREAT

I have spent many weeks in Medjugorje. Such gifts! Such grace! The presence of the Holy Spirit! It stays with you: all the memories of the place. Almost always you can find pilgrims around the grounds of the parish church of Saint James and the parish house. Often, especially during the late spring, summer, and early fall, great crowds assemble.

The church, quite large for a parish church, nevertheless often cannot hold all the people who come for the evening rosary and the Mass. They spill over outside the church. Frequently even the special wooden benches set up outside cannot accommodate everyone. Now it is being replaced by an immense pavilion, across the whole front of St. James Church. It, too, is proving to be inadequate.

People come in such large numbers because they believe that the mother of Jesus has specially chosen that place and that parish and that church, that she has visited it in a special way, and that her special presence continues there. And where Mary is, in a special way, so is Jesus. So people come, looking for God, looking for the Lord. They did the same during Jesus' lifetime here on earth. They came looking for God and looking for healing.

Sometimes the crowding at Medjugorje can become intense. When Our Lady appeared daily in the auxiliary sacristy in the church, and later when she appeared in a room in the parish house, often crowds struggled to get into the sacristy or the room to be present when Mary came to the young people. It could get hectic. Even now the crowding into the parish church in the evening can get oppressive.

And yet, with all the crowds and the crowding, perhaps partly because of that and partly because all have come for the same purposes, you can find at Medjugorje a wonderful spirit of helpfulness, of cooperation, of love—among the milling crowds of foreigners, Croatians, and villagers; and in the homes where most pilgrims stay.

You do not know everyone. You may know no one. But you do know that you are together with everyone in the Lord.

The healings that take place at Medjugorje are signs of the presence of the power of God. They increase our faith. And they show the quality of the Lord's love:

The Blessed Virgin Mary at Medjugorje has frequently called us to greater faith. She prays for greater faith for each of us, and I can pray with her to Jesus, "Lord, increase my faith!"

What is faith? Faith means not only believing the truths that God has revealed. It includes that, but faith goes beyond agreeing to the truth of Christianity. Faith means believing in Jesus Christ, adhering to Him, hanging on to Him. And in Him is contained all truth; He is the Truth as well as the Way and the Life.

Faith means accepting Jesus' personal call to a close union with Him, to discipleship, to friendship, to follow Him wholeheartedly. And faith is a gift.

Our Lady at the beginning of her daily visits to Medjugorje identified herself as the Queen of Peace. She applies that title to herself now, in our times, when there is so little peace in the world.

And she calls us to pray for peace: peace in the world, among peoples and nations; peace within nations among opposed parties and factions; peace in our own cities and towns and regions. And peace in our families; and peace in our hearts.

Peace begins at home, in my own heart. It begins and continues with my continuous conversion from sin and to Jesus, with my acceptance of His call and of the increase in faith that He offers me, and with my prayer and fasting.

Medjugorje is truly a retreat. We all need to make it. All of us. As a retreat, it's a conversion that we need to live every day, the rest of our lives. You don't have to go there to do it. He, and His Mother, will come to wherever you are.

ROBERT FARICY, S.J.
(Fr. Faricy is currently re-locating
to Europe and the return to teaching.)

(Note: The above taken from "Medjugorje Retreat," yet to be published. Fr. Faricy, with Sr. Lucy Rooney, have also authored several other books on Medjugorje.)

Chapter 22

THE MESSAGE OF MARIAN APPARITIONS

In the Encyclical "The Great Sign," Pope Paul VI stated: "Our era may well be called the Marian era." (May 13, 1967).

An unprecedented number of Marian apparitions in our times has ushered in the "Age of Mary." St. Louis de Montfort predicted that "God wishes His holy Mother should be more known, more honored, and more loved at present than ever before."

This knowledge, honor and love of Mary has been enhanced worldwide through her apparitions which manifest her role in salvation history. Her message reaffirms the Gospel message. She reveals no new doctrine or teaching. Although these are known as private revelations, they contain public messages intended for today's historical situation, having an immediacy and urgency for our instruction and admonition.

At Lourdes, the Blessed Mother set the pattern and purpose of her appearances. Revealing herself, *I am the Immaculate Conception,* she urged, *penitence, penitence,* the rosary, prayer for sinners and a firm faith which she encouraged through signs and cures by the miraculous waters at the grotto. The message of Lourdes was reaffirmed by the momentous event of Fatima (the miracle of the sun,

Oct. 13, 1917), the only predicted public miracle performed so that mankind would believe.

Apparitions indicate the constant and urgent message for mankind's conversion and peace. Lourdes and Fatima have the Church's approval; Garabandal and Medjugorje have not received official approbation. Since these revelations contain prophetic elements, the Church waits for their possible fulfillment before passing judgment on them; for example, thirteen years elapsed before the approval of Fatima even though 70,000 people witnessed the miracle of the sun. Nonetheless, the Church grants us an option to believe in non-approved apparitions, provided that they contain nothing contrary to Catholic faith or morals.

It is important to maintain the distinction between the authenticity of the apparitions and the teaching of their messages. While the local bishops of Garabandal and of Medjugorje have expressed denial of the supernatural origin of the alleged apparitions in their respective dioceses, they have affirmed the soundness of the messages. This was expressly stated in 1963, by Bishop Eugenio Beitia, of Garabandal; and likewise by Bishop Zanic, who after voicing objections to the divine nature of events at Medjugorje, asserted the validity of the messages and at the same time qualified his objections that "in no way indicate a final judgment on the part of competent authority."

However, the question of why Mary comes to Medjugorje deserves a direct answer. From the messages from Mary to the six youngsters receiving the visions, we understand that Mary comes as catechist, a teacher, to restate the basic truths of our religion and to clear up the confusion in religious education. She comes as Scripture exegete to demythologize the demythologizers. She comes as Eucharistic promoter to repair the harm and neglect of Jesus in the Blessed Sacrament.

The seers have said that the highlight of their day is not the apparition, but the daily Mass. In fact, the center of Medjugorje for the pilgrims is the evening Mass. Mary comes to Medjugorje especially as our weeping and sorrowful mother, pleading for a return of all children to her Divine Son. She is the Immaculate and Sorrowful Mother—the first title was freely given to her by God, the second she received "the old-fashioned way, she earned it," at the foot of the Cross where, by her compassion, she shared in the Passion of Christ for our redemption.

The visionaries are reported as having seen Mary weeping by the Cross. Mary comes to win sinners back to God. She begs them to accept her message of peace by means of faith, prayer, fasting, reconciliation and conversion. In addition, they have been asked by Our Lady to announce this message to the villagers, the pilgrims and the world. The people have responded to these requests in remarkable numbers these past seven years: thousands present for daily Mass; over a million have gone to confession here; tens of thousands have acquired the practice of Friday fasting on just bread and water; millions are daily reciting the Rosary because of Medjugorje; innumerable conversions have taken place.

In the meantime, we may prudently follow the advice of Lucy of Fatima, Conchita of Garabandal, and the six youths of Medjugorje, who all in effect, state that it is of no use to believe in the apparitions if we do not observe the message. But, it is urgent that we follow the message even if we do not believe in the apparitions. While we may reasonably question or deny credence in apparitions, it would seem rash to ignore their messages, particularly that of Fatima, for as Pope Pius XII wrote: "The time of doubting Fatima is passed," and as Pope John Paul II said: "Fatima is more urgent and more relevant now than ever before."

FR. PETER TOSCANI, O.S.A.
St. Nicholas Church
Philadelphia, PA

(Fr. Toscani is an established writer, including a number of articles on Our Lady, and Medjugorje. His article, "Medjugorje Overview" appeared in the Homiletic & Pastoral Review, May, 1988)

Chapter 23

FORMING
OUR
CHRISTIAN VISION

We are well aware of the content of Our Lady's messages at Medjugorje. It is clear that she desires to bring us to a deep conversion to Christ and His Gospel, through faith, prayer and fasting, the Sacraments, etc. Yet, given the way people often compartmentalize their lives, these elements may be taken in isolation from the broad vision of the Gospel as a whole. They may be seen as duties to fulfill, instead of what they really are: a way of life!

I think that Our Lady is trying to instill in us a radically Christian "vision," a mind-set, a world view, in which each of the elements of her message falls naturally into place. This kind of vision of what the Christian life is meant to be, is outlined in the Sermon on the Mount, and in such texts as Romans 12, and Colossians 3.

If we hear the word of God and keep it; if we meditate on the messages of the Madonna and live them; we will begin to develop this vision to rely on faith, as the means through which we interpret the events of our lives. Thus, we become more fully transformed and sanctified.

We then will pray not only at a set time, for our whole life, with all of its daily activities, will be permeated with a prayerful spirit. We will not only go to Confession and receive the Holy Eucharist on a regular basis; our whole way of thinking and of approaching life's problems, will flow from the awareness of Jesus' faithful love and indwelling presence. Our constant reference point will be our relationship with God and Our Lady.

Likewise, we will not only set aside certain times for fasting; our hunger for God and our detachment from the pleasures of the world, will be an ongoing reality. These are just a few examples of the way individual acts are integrated into a whole comprehensive vision of life. We need to see the entire vision, not an isolated part of it.

It is time to go beyond the minimum. We cannot think: "what is the least I can do and still be following the messages?" I believe that Our Lady wants us to live our lives wholly centered on her Son, Jesus, with the grace of the Holy Spirit as our natural environment, as water is for the fish. This call to a deep life in Christ, does not set before us some inaccessible ideal of sanctity or mystical experience, but it does require daily faithfulness to the word of God. It means taking the Gospel seriously.

When our lives are grounded in this genuinely Christian vision, we won't have to worry about keeping track of our sacrifices piecemeal, because our lives will be an *unending sacrifice of praise*. (*Heb.* 13:15). Love does not count the cost, but rejoices in giving. How could we ever say, "I have prayed enough today," when we realize that we owe everything to the Lord?

Our Lady said that if we knew all the graces God was giving us, we would pray unceasingly. Prayer must become an interior necessity, making us realize (hopefully to our great delight), that we cannot live without God. We are not our own. We have been redeemed at the price of Jesus' blood. (*1 Cor.* 6:20). Each one of us has been "sent" by God to carry out *His* will, for His glory and the salvation of all.

Mary does not come saying, "Pray, pray, pray," just because she is the Mother of God, and, well, we expect her to say things like that. She has a vision of God and of eternity that we do not yet have. She is testifying, as one who knows. This is the lady of Genesis, the *Lady clothed with the sun.* What she calls us to do, is the way to eternal life.

Mary is a Mother who is filled with immeasurable love and concern for her children. Blessed are those who give her joy through obedience, and a loving response to her call, for she will see to it that God gives them eternal joy in Heaven. We need to see that whole Christian vision she is giving to us. It's a reaffirmation of the teachings of her Son.

FR. JOSEPH HOMICK
Mt. Tabor Monastery
Redwood Valley, CA

Chapter 24

SURRENDER YOURSELVES

For seven years now Mary has been with her children through Medjugorje, and for the past four years, has been giving weekly or monthly messages for the world. She brings us another this month, June 25th, 1988.

This message that came over the anniversary date of the apparitions, follows the messages we have been getting for the past 8 or 9 months. Mary is calling us to a deeper surrender. Here is how she expresses that theme in this message:

Dear Children, I am calling you to that love which is loyal and pleasing to God. Little children, love bears everything bitter and difficult for the sake of Jesus, who is love. Therefore, dear children, pray that God comes to your aid, not however, according to your desires, but according to His love. Surrender yourselves to God so that He may heal you, console you and forgive everything inside you which is a hindrance on the way of love. In this way, God can move your life and you will grow in love. Dear children, glorify God with a hymn of love so that God's love may be able to grow in you

96

day by day to its fullness. Thank you for having responded to my call.

I am calling you to that love which is loyal and pleasing to God. Mary focuses first of all on love. But it is a love that is "loyal." Loyal love means one that supports, stands by through thick and thin, respects, understands. Loyalty is not putting judgments on others. She calls us to this in-depth love as someone who knows, who has been there.

She continues in stating that this loyal love has to accept and bear with what is bitter and difficult. Accept the bitter or difficult, not because we desire difficulty, but because of the loyal love it produces. She constantly calls us to recognize that Jesus is love, and that He comes to us as the God of Love, seeking our loyalty.

We need to spend more time just drinking that in, the many ways that God loves us. I have found it is very important to grow in gratitude, to grow in that quality where I recognize the love of God. It is empowering, because, if I can do that when things are going well, then I will be able to hold onto Jesus' hand when things are difficult or bitter.

She says, *Pray that God comes to your aid, not however according to your desires, but according to His love.*

The request is, pray that God comes to my aid, but, not the way I am praying, not the way I am demanding, not the way I would like Him to come, but the way His own perfect love of me dictates. Usually we complain if He doesn't come the way we want. Let God respond in His way.

We tend to experience it in the same way a child often receives direction or guidance from a parent; as something terrible. "Mom and Dad don't love me, or won't listen to me. They won't let me go out and play in the street. Why do I have to this or that." We sometimes see from a child's perspective; but as a parent, we see the way we reach out to protect and encourage; we instill traits, responsibilities. God reaches out and responds to us according to His love. Our failure is that we need to be convinced of that love first, so that we can trust it.

So now we come to the heart of the message. *Surrender yourselves to God.*

The word "surrender" has been coming up regularly for seven or eight months. What does surrender mean to you? You can surrender, like to an enemy who overpowers you. You can surrender "to something" when you feel helpless, powerless, just give-in. But there is also the surrender of two people who trust one another; that thing that St. Paul spoke about in a married couple—be submissive to one another. That's surrender. Submission because of the love of the other. Mary states Jesus is loyal, and He wants us to have a loyal love, and we need to surrender ourselves to Him, to allow Him to do fantastic things with us, and for us. Surrender, so that He can heal.

I have found that if I have something that needs healing, but I keep it all inside, I can't be healed. I find that in working with couples, the time of healing usually happens when one of the spouses can submit to the love of the other spouse.

Granted, yes, I am still hurt, and I know I am hurt, but I reach out. And Mary is saying that when we can surrender to God, when we can place ourselves totally in His hands, His love can begin to heal us in a new way.

I have also found that many times I cannot be healed because I am harboring anger, or I am harboring a hurt, and I will not surrender it to anyone. Jesus wants to console, uplift, forgive, to give us the deepest experience of His love, which is forgiveness. But we cannot experience that if we do not submit or surrender ourselves to Him in some way.

It is beginning to be more clear to me how powerfully Mary is calling us into the heart of Jesus. That is the focus of the Fatima messages as well: to enter in, to listen to, to be with the Immaculate Heart, so that she can bring us into the Sacred Heart of her Son. And we enter that by surrendering.

She tells us further, that God wants to forgive everything inside of us, which is a hindrance on the way to love. In other words, the purpose of His healing, the purpose of His forgiveness, His consoling, is so that you and I can come to love in a new way. Reach out to someone in love and you experience God.

The heart of the Medjugorje message is the same thing Jesus said when He began His public ministry. It is leaving sin and being converted. Convert your lives. The conversion comes from surrendering to Jesus, by surrendering to the Gospel, to love, by living it.

God speaks to us all the time in the circumstances of our lives. We seldom see it. We keep asking for an answer, a direction, and He keeps answering us through a spouse, or child, a neighbor, and we can't see it, we cannot hear it. And very often, it is through a person that we might be having difficulty with, because He wants to free us of the hurt and the anger, the sin, that blocks the love.

There is a Psalm that priests say every day—Psalm 95. It contains a phrase, *If today you hear His voice, harden not your heart.* The greatest problem many of us have is that we have hardened the heart. Surrender, listen more deeply. Mary wants for God to move our lives. She continues in the message, *Glorify God with a hymn of love.* She asks that we allow God's love to grow in us day by day, and she asks us to do it by praising and glorifying God. Offer a prayer of praise.

FR. ALFRED WINSHMAN, S.J.
Loyola House, Boston, MA

(from a homily to the Queen of Peace Prayer Group, on the meaning of the message of June 25th, 1988.)

Fr. Winshman is being permanently assigned to Loyola House in a Marian/Medjugorje ministry

Chapter 25

LIFE IS LIKE A FLOWER

On April 6, 1985, Our Lady gave the seers of Medjugorje an image to help them in living their lives. It was the image of a flower. She said, *You all know flowers. A flower must blossom and every part of the flower is very important for the flower.*

What could be simpler than a flower! What is more familiar to us than a flower!

Beauty Blossoms With Love

Every flower is beautiful. No matter if it is a rose or a dandelion, an orchid or a violet, a dahlia or a daisy, an aster or an azalea. A flower—any flower—is just beautiful.

Once Jelena asked Mary, "Our Lady, why are you so beautiful?"

Our Lady answered, *I am beautiful because I love. If you want to become beautiful, love and you will not need the mirror so much.*

Heaven is a place so exceedingly filled with beauty and happiness because it is filled with the love of God, and with people filled with love.

Hell is the opposite because it is made up of hate, and people filled with hate.

St. Bernadette of Lourdes said, "Every moment that I live I

shall spend in loving." Our Lady, at Medjugorje, in her me
to the world May 25, 1988 said, *I wish that you love all man*
with my love. Our beauty will flower if we become loving pers

A Beautiful Bouquet

No two flowers are alike. Each flower has its own beau
It makes no difference if it be tall as the sunflower or low
as the humble violet—every flower is unique. So are you!

"Person" means somebody unique, somebody distinct from
everybody else. As no two fingerprints are alike, so no two persons are exactly alike. Therefore, envy should never have a place
in our lives. Each of us is a person; somebody nobody else is.
Each of us has a role to play in life that no one else can play.
As in a symphony, each player is important, so in the symphony
of life each one of us is important. If you do not become what
you are meant to be, do not give what you alone can give, if
you do not play your part in the symphony of life, then the
world will be the poorer for this.

No matter how many different flowers there are in a bouquet, no matter how much each flower differs in color from
the other, there is no conflict—just beautiful harmony. It is
a flower's way of calling us to live in harmony; to make life
a beautiful bouquet of unity in variety.

Grow In Goodness And Love

To grow into a beautiful flower takes time. Nature never acts
in haste. It takes 100 years to complete an olive tree. Allow yourself the time to grow. Don't let failures, falls, lapses uproot you.
As Bishop Fulton Sheen once said, "A saint is a sinner who
keeps on trying."

The theme of the Book of Revelation is "faithful endurance";
the crown is given to the one who perseveres to the end. You
can break bad habits by good ones. It takes many grains of
wheat to make the bread. It takes many good acts to make a
good habit.

That is why, in Medjugorje, Our Lady teaches us the need
for persevering prayer. In every apparition she asks for prayer.
But, on April 25, 1987, she begged the children (and each of

ray with your hearts. Persevering prayer is ... which to bloom.

..., we must first remove two obstacles to prayer:

...turn your back on God; to pray is to turn your ... to Him. But you can't face two directions at the ... Therefore, to pray well, you have to get rid of sin. ... ible ailment. And it gets inside us. In fact, the vowel ... ddle of the word "sin" is "I."

... cond obstacle to prayer is worry. You can't pray and ... t the same time. Worry crowds out prayer. Worry is fear ... future, of an impending evil. The future belongs to God. ... as a No Trespassing sign there. When you trespass into ... future, the penalty is worry. Someone said: "Sorrow looks ... ck, worry looks ahead, and Faith looks up!"

Prayer is a meeting with Our Lord. Our big sin today is that we have no time for God. The food for us as the "flower" is prayer. The important thing is, you have to take the time to do it.

Man's days, wrote the Psalmist, *are like a flower of the field; the wind sweeps over him and he is gone, and his place knows him no more.* (*Ps.* 103:15-16). To the children at Medjugorje, Our Lady said, *Don't forget that your life is fleeting like a spring flower which today is wondrously beautiful but tomorrow has vanished.* (3-25-88)

We therefore, are a pilgrim people. We have not here a lasting city; we look for one that is to come. Life on earth is like staying at a hotel; remember, it is not home.

In the Divine Office, we pray: "Eternal God, for whom a thousand years are like the passing day, help us to remember life is like a flower which blossoms in the morning but withers in the evening."

Eternal Father, help us to live in the light of this truth.

FR. ALBERT J.M. SHAMON
St. Isaac Jogues Parish
Fleming, NY

(Note: Fr. Shamon is the author of the booklet, "Our Lady Teaches About Prayer in Medjugorje," available from The Riehle Foundation.)